Editor
Lorin Klistoff, M.A.

Editorial Manager
Karen Goldfluss, M.S. Ed.

Editor-in-Chief
Sharon Coan, M.S. Ed.

Cover Artist
Sue Fullam

Art Coordinator
Denice Adorno

Creative Director
Elayne Roberts

Imaging
James Edward Grace

Product Manager
Phil Garcia

Publisher
Mary D. Smith, M.S. Ed.

STANDARDIZED TEST PRACTICE FOR 7TH GRADE

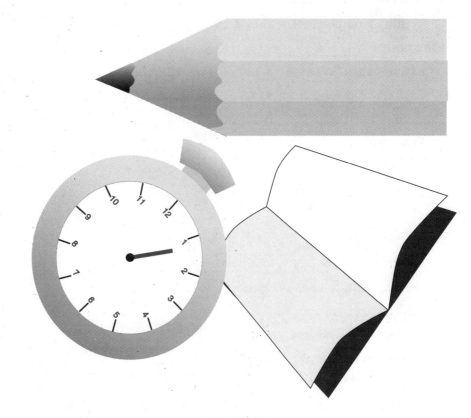

Author

Charles J. Shields

Teacher Created Resources, Inc.
6421 Industry Way
Westminster, CA 92683
www.teachercreated.com

©2000 Teacher Created Resources, Inc.
Reprinted, 2005
Made in U.S.A.
ISBN-1-57690-682-5

Table of Contents

You have undoubtedly given plenty of tests during your years of teaching—unit tests, pop quizzes, final exams, and yes, standardized tests. As a professional educator, you know that standardized tests have taken on an importance greater than any of the others.

No one who understands children and the nature of learning would argue that a standardized test provides a measure of a child's understanding, a teacher's effectiveness, or a school's performance. It is a statistical snapshot of a group of children on a particular day. And there is no "generic child." Take a look at a girl named Joanna, for instance. Reluctant to speak during discussions or participate in group work, she's a whiz at taking tests and scores high on formal tests. However, Dion, in the seat beside her, is creative but impulsive. He dawdles during timed tests and sometimes fills in the wrong answer section. His score? It is no more a true indication of his ability than his doodles of motorcycle-riding monsters in the margins of his papers. You are probably thinking of a Joanna or a Dion in your class right now.

However, schools must be accountable to their communities. Moreover, issues of equity and opportunity for children require that some method of checking all students' progress as objectively as possible be administered annually or even semi-annually. As a result, at the insistence of parents, school boards, state legislatures, and national commissions, standardized tests and their results are receiving more attention now than at any other time during the last 35 years.

The purpose of this book is to help you and your students get better results on standardized tests. The exercises are grade-specific and based on the most recent versions of these testing instruments:

The California Achievement Tests
The Iowa Tests of Basic Skills
The Comprehensive Tests of Basic Skills
The Stanford Achievement Tests
The Metropolitan Achievement Tests
The Texas Assessment of Academic Skills

Exercise materials designed for this book reflect skills from curricula, grade-level tests, and test taking from the California Academic Standards Commission, the New York State Testing Program for Elementary and Intermediate Grades, the Texas Essential Knowledge and Skills program, and the Board of Education for the Commonwealth of Virginia. Your students can expect to meet again on widely used standardized tests most of the content in this book and the style in which questions are posed.

About the Practice Tests

You will notice several things right away about the exercises.

1. The tests are arranged by curricular topics: grammar, reading comprehension, or geometry, for example.

2. The exercises are short enough that you can integrate them into your teaching day. If you spend 20 minutes daily on test taking over several weeks as you approach a test date, your students will build confidence and increase their knowledge base in preparation for the actual test. Becoming familiar with testing formats and practicing on sample questions is one of the most effective ways to improve scores.

3. Examples of student-constructed responses to problems and questions have been included. Students must write, draw, or show their work to get credit for their answers.

Each section of the book—Language Arts, Mathematics, Science, Social Studies, Fine Arts, Computers and Technology—begins with a short lesson for students about answering the questions in that section and includes a list of test-taking tips. It would be a good idea to have your students take turns reading portions of the lesson aloud so you can emphasize key suggestions.

Ways to Increase Students' Confidence

- Downplay the importance of how many right answers versus how many wrong answers your students give. These exercises generally have the same purpose as drills in sports—to improve players' ability through regular practice. Fill the role of coach as students learn to hit the long ball.

- Give credit for reasonable answers. Encourage students to explain why they answered as they did. Praise thoughtfulness and good guesses. Surprise them by giving partial credit because their logic is persuasive. On some state-designed tests, credit is given for "almost right" answers.

- Promote in your classroom a positive, relaxed feeling about test taking. It might be wise, for example, to put off administering a planned practice from this booklet if your students are anxious or feeling overwhelmed about something. Use a little psychology in strengthening the association in their minds between test taking and opportunities to feel pleased about themselves.

The following pages provide a list of the basic skills embedded in the tests in this book.

Language Arts

Reading

Construct meaning from literary, informational, and practical texts.

Read literary materials with complex characters, settings, and episodes.

Read informational and practical materials with complex vocabulary, concepts, and formats.

Recognize the characteristics of expository (point of view) text.

Recognize coherence, logic, and organization in expository (point of view) text.

Recognize meter as a characteristic of poetry.

Identify plot and sub-plot in novels and other literary texts.

Recognize the poet's use of language devices such as sound, diction, and symbolism.

Writing

Write point-of-view pieces that have a coherent, logical, and organized structure.

Use concrete images and vivid descriptions in expository (point-of-view) writing.

Revise by rearranging, deleting, or adding new ideas and/or paragraphs.

Write expository (point-of-view) texts that provide sufficient, related, elaborated reasons to support a position.

Express main idea and use details in argumentative writing.

Use a range of vocabulary, grammatical structures, forms, and modes effectively and appropriately for purpose and audience.

Recognize and use parts of speech correctly.

Mathematics

Rational and Real Numbers

Compare and order rational numbers in meaningful context.

Express whole numbers in scientific notation; convert scientific notation to standard form.

Use exponential notation to express prime factorization of numbers less than 100.

Use estimation techniques with rational numbers.

Estimate and solve problems using ratios, proportions, and percent.

Apply concepts of ratio, proportion, and percent to real-life situations such as consumer applications, science, and social studies.

Use real-world examples or models to represent multiplication and division of integers, then record and explain procedures used.

Geometry

Use geometric models to develop the meaning of the square and the positive square root of a number.

Relate concepts of ratio, proportion, and percent in meaningful context.

Demonstrate an understanding and use properties and relationships of geometry.

Use the properties and relationships of geometry to solve problems.

Identify applications of geometry in the environment.

Graph shapes and congruent figures on a coordinate plane.

Mathematics *(cont.)*

Pre-Algebra

Demonstrate an understanding of patterns and pre-algebra.

Describe, extend, analyze, and create a wide variety of patterns to investigate relationships and solve problems.

Use the concept of operations with variables.

Solve simple linear equations.

Investigate and evaluate algebraic expressions using mental calculations, pencil and paper, and calculators where appropriate.

Measurement

Demonstrate an understanding and use of measurement.

Calculate surface area for rectangular solids and cylinders.

Calculate the volume of prisms and cylinders.

Statistics and Probability

Demonstrate an understanding and use of graphing, statistics, and probability.

Analyze data.

Find the probability of simple events.

Science

General Science

Atmospheric Studies

Explain the composition, properties, and structure of the atmosphere.

Identify atmospheric properties that can be studied to predict atmospheric conditions.

Geology

Identify the earth's structure.

Understand the nature of forces that change the external features of the earth.

Biology and Cells

Analyze structures, functions, and processes within plants and animals.

Compare life functions of protists.

Analyze human body systems.

Relate disease to biological hazards.

Explain the significance of chromosomes, genes, and DNA in cell reproduction and their relationship to inherited characteristics.

Properties of Matter

Classify substances based on their properties: elements, compounds, and mixtures.

Relate state of matter to the arrangement and motion of atoms or molecules.

Classify objects based on characteristics: density, boiling/melting points, and solubility.

Describe quantities related to chemical/physical changes within a system: temperature, volume, mass, precipitation, and gas production.

Reading

Analyze the role of environment.

Social Studies

World History
Ancient Egypt
Ancient Greece
Ancient Rome

World Geography

United States History
Early Exploration
Pre-Revolutionary America
The American Revolution
The Constitution
Slavery
The Election of 1860
The Westward Movement

Fine Arts

Music
Identify simple musical forms.

Compare in two or more arts how the characteristic materials of each art can be used to transform similar events, scenes, emotions, or ideas into works of art.

Classify by genre and style a variety of musical works.

Dance
Understand the concept of improvisation.

Understand the concept of composition.

Understand the role of dance in various cultures.

Make connections between dance and healthful living.

Theater
Recognize what drama is and how it happens.

Recognize unique characteristics of the dramatic script.

Understand the difference between actor and character.

Understand and analyze dramatic elements found in theatre, film, television, and electronic media presentations.

Computers and Technology
Demonstrate an understanding of copyright by citing sources of copyrighted materials in papers, projects, and multimedia presentations.

Demonstrate knowledge and skills in the use of computer and other technologies.

Search and sort information using more than one criterion and explain strategies used to find information.

Choose charts, tables, or graphs to best represent data and state reason.

Evaluate the information from electronic sources as to validity, appropriateness, content, and usefulness.

Lesson 1: Minding the Minutes

The purpose of this lesson is to help you learn how to answer the most questions you can on a standardized test.

A standardized test is timed. It is another way of trying to make the test fair. It would not be fair to allow some students to spend an hour solving a dozen one-step math problems—which is much longer than necessary—and a second group of students to spend only 15 minutes. Would it be clear who understood the problems better? No, it would not be a fair or an accurate measure of the students' abilities.

Keep in mind that you get credit for the number of questions you answer correctly. The more questions you answer correctly, the higher your score. Keeping this in mind, what do you think you should do when you have a limited amount of time to answer a lot of questions?

To answer this question, imagine what you would do in another situation. You are about to play a game outside. In this game, you have 10 minutes to gather all the pieces of candy you can. The pieces have been hidden in the grass, in the bushes, and next to stones. Some of them are easy to see; some are well-hidden. Now, what would you do?

You would probably run around and pick up all the pieces you could see right away. If you still had time, you could go back and search for the pieces that are well-hidden. But remember—the idea is to get as many pieces of candy as you can. So go for the easy ones first!

Believe it or not, the same strategy works on a standardized test. See for yourself. Here are three math questions that you must finish with only half of a minute left on the test.

1.
$$\frac{2}{6}$$
$$+ \frac{1}{6}$$

   (A) $1/6$
   (B) $3/12$
   (C) $3/6$
   (D) 3
   (E) none of these

   Fill in the correct circle.

   Ⓐ   Ⓑ   Ⓒ   Ⓓ   Ⓔ

2.
$$\frac{2}{7} = \frac{?}{35}$$

   (F) 7
   (G) 5
   (H) 10
   (J) 11
   (K) none of these

   Fill in the correct circle.

   Ⓕ   Ⓖ   Ⓗ   Ⓙ   Ⓚ

3.
$$\frac{3}{8} + \frac{1}{4} =$$

   (A) $2/4$
   (B) $2/8$
   (C) $4/12$
   (D) $4/8$
   (E) none of these

   Fill in the correct circle.

   Ⓐ   Ⓑ   Ⓒ   Ⓓ   Ⓔ

Lesson 1: Minding the Minutes *(cont.)*

You might be able to answer all three problems on the previous page, but if you had to choose, which would you skip? You would probably not try problem 2 since it looks like it would take the longest amount of time to solve.

What if there are 25 math problems on one part of a test and you skipped six of them because they looked like they would take longer to solve? How do you remind yourself to go back? *Put a little check mark on your answer sheet next to each problem you skipped.* If there is time, you can go back and work on the harder problems.

Here is one more example in which you might have to skip questions on a test, but the choice is a little different. What if there are two reading passages on a test—one has four questions after it, and the other one has eight? You think you only have time to read one of the passages. Which one should you choose?

Choose the one with eight questions after it. Maybe you will only have time to answer six of the eight questions, but you will probably get more of them right than if you read the other passage, answered the four questions, and then were reading the second passage when you ran out of time.

Whenever you can, answer correctly as many questions as you can on a standardized test. That's the smart way to mind the minutes.

Lesson 2: Guessing Correctly

This lesson will explain to you that it is possible to answer a question correctly, even if you're just guessing. The secret is narrowing your choices.

Sometimes you will be faced with a really difficult multiple-choice question. It might be that
- you do not understand the question very well.
- you do not understand the answer choices.
- you simply do not know the answer at all.

What should you do? Guess? Yes, you should guess. But you can increase the chance of choosing the correct answer by using a few strategies.

"Best-Guess" Strategies

1. Always make sure to read all the choices.

Do not jump at the first one that looks like it might be right. Here is an example:

Which is the largest city?

    (A) Los Angeles

    (B) Detroit

    (C) Atlanta

    (D) New York

Fill in the correct circle.

Ⓐ   Ⓑ   Ⓒ   Ⓓ

Lesson 2: Guessing Correctly *(cont.)*

"Best-Guess" Strategies *(cont.)*

Maybe you do not know which is the largest city, but you do know that (A) "Los Angeles" is bigger than (B) "Detroit," so you choose (A) "Los Angeles" and go on to the next question. But wait! It is important to read all the choices. In fact, (D) "New York" is the largest city. You might have guessed between (A) "Los Angeles" or (D) "New York" if you had read all the possible answers. To be a good guesser, you must read every choice and think about each of them, one at a time. If you are the kind of tester who always reads all the choices before choosing one, then you are doing the right thing.

2. Eliminate the answer choices that are plainly wrong.

Here is an example of a social studies question you might find on a test. Choose the correct term.

How can the president stop a law that has been passed by Congress?

(A) politics

(B) capital

(C) veto

(D) arrest

Fill in the correct circle.

Ⓐ   Ⓑ   Ⓒ   Ⓓ

Think carefully about this situation. Choice (A) "politics" is something like "business" or "teaching"— it is a profession. How could it be used to stop anything? Next, (B) "capital" is usually a place, like a state capital. It could not be used to stop a process like passing a law. What about (D) "arrest"? People do get stopped when they are put "under arrest," but this is a law being talked about, not people, so (D) "arrest" is probably not the correct answer. That leaves (C) "veto" as the most likely choice because each of the other choices does not quite fit for some reason. If you chose (C) "veto," you would be right.

3. Look carefully for clues about how the word is used.

On some tests, you might run across a reading passage that has vocabulary words that you do not know. Here is an example of such a reading passage.

In *The Goats* (1987), Brock Cole's first novel, Howie Mitchell and Laura Golden meet at Tall Pine, a summer camp. They recognize each other as outcasts. "I'm socially retarded for my age," Laura tells Howie. "Yeah. Me too," Howie replies. But deep down, neither of them believes those statements. When a cruel practical joke leaves them abandoned on an island, they seize the opportunity to test their <u>self-reliance</u> and independence. They escape from the island, steer clear of their camp, and make do for themselves. They remain on the run until they are confident they have new identities they can be proud of.

Based on the passage you read, what is the meaning of the word *self-reliance*?

(A) personal courage

(B) tools

(C) meanness

(D) depending on oneself

Fill in the correct circle.

Ⓐ   Ⓑ   Ⓒ   Ⓓ

Lesson 2: Guessing Correctly *(cont.)*

"Best-Guess" Strategies *(cont.)*

In this case, if you do not know the meaning of the word *self-reliance*, you need to look carefully for clues about how the word is used. The passage says Howie and Laura were abandoned on an island and used the "opportunity to test their self-reliance and independence." Why would they test their (C) "meanness" in such a situation? That does not make much sense. And nothing is said about them having (B) "tools." If they had tools, it would not have been a "cruel practical joke" to leave them abandoned on an island. "Tools" is not a good choice. They might have tested their (A) "personal courage," but the passage also said they "make do for themselves" which suggests (D) "depending on oneself." So both (A) and (D) are likely choices, but at least you have eliminated two of the four choices. Now you have a fifty-fifty chance of getting the answer correct. Which do you choose, (A) or (D)? The answer is (D) "depending on oneself."

4. **For a math problem, you can use estimating to help you when you are not sure of the answer.**

Now try this problem.

The choir practiced for 2 $\frac{3}{4}$ hours on Saturday and 3 $\frac{2}{3}$ hours on Sunday. How much was the total time?

Fill in the correct circle.

(A) 4 $\frac{3}{4}$ hours
(B) 5 $\frac{17}{12}$ hours
(C) 5 $\frac{7}{8}$ hours
(D) 6 $\frac{5}{12}$ hours

(A)　(B)　(C)　(D)

Maybe this problem gives you trouble because you have difficulty with fractions. Use estimation to help you make your best guess.

Looking at the whole numbers in the problem, the choir practiced 2 hours + 3 hours which totals 5 hours. Five is more than (A) 4 $\frac{3}{4}$ hours. You know that is true even without adding the fractions. (A) cannot be correct. Next, the mixed number (B) 5 $\frac{17}{12}$ is strange. Have you ever seen a mixed number in which the numerator of the fraction is larger than the denominator? (B) is probably not correct either. (C) 5 $\frac{7}{8}$ is a possibility, but look closely; 8 is not a common denominator of $\frac{3}{4}$ and $\frac{2}{3}$. How could you get an answer like (C) 5 $\frac{7}{8}$? That leaves (D) 6 $\frac{5}{12}$.

If you guessed (D) even without doing the problem, you would be right. You did some quick estimating to solve the problem.

Remember to use these four strategies:
- Make sure to read all the answer choices.
- Eliminate choices that are plainly wrong.
- Look for clues about how a word is used.
- Estimate the answer.

You are sure to raise your test scores if you practice guessing correctly.

Introduction

The language arts section of standardized tests always involves a lot of reading. There are short questions, too, of course, but quite often you must read a paragraph or a long passage to answer the questions.

Here's the Idea

To answer your best on the language arts sections, you must be able to do the following:

1. Identify main ideas.
2. Recognize important details or clues.
3. Draw conclusions on your own.

Before we look at each of the three skills, read the following tips that apply to taking any test, whether it is in language arts, mathematics, science, social studies, fine arts, or computers and technology. These tips will be repeated because they are important!

Test-Taking Tips

- **Read directions carefully before marking any test questions**, even though you have done that kind of test before. You may think you already know what the directions say, but don't ignore them—read them over. If you do not understand the directions, raise your hand and ask for help. Although your teacher must read the directions exactly as they are written, the teacher can make sure you understand what the directions mean.

- **Follow instructions.** Pay close attention to the sample exercises. They will help you understand what the items on the test will be like and how to mark your answer sheet properly.

- **Read the entire question and all the answer choices.** Do not stop reading when you have found a correct answer. Choices D or E may read "B and D" or "all of the above" or "none of the above." On some tests, two answers are both correct. You need to read all the answer choices before marking your answer.

- **For long reading passages, read the questions first so you know what to look for.** If you read the questions first, you will find information in the passage that answers questions.

- **Remember that taking a test is not a race!** There are no prizes for finishing first. Use all of the time provided for the test. If you have time left over, check your answers.

Try and Discuss

Now let's discuss the same three skills (*identifying main ideas*, *recognizing important details or clues*, and *drawing conclusions on your own*) for language arts tests.

Take a look at the question below.

Which one names the whole group?

(A) Earth

(B) Mercury

(C) Pluto

(D) solar system

(E) orbits

Fill in the correct circle.

Ⓐ   Ⓑ   Ⓒ   Ⓓ   Ⓔ

One of these words includes all of the others. It is (D) "solar system." The planets—Earth, Mercury, and Pluto—are all part of the solar system, and all the planets travel in an orbit in the solar system.

The main idea of a paragraph is just like that—it is an idea that names all of the other ideas in the paragraph by making them one group. You will be asked to identify main ideas on language arts tests. You also may be asked, "What would be a good title for this?" which is another way of asking, "What is the main idea?"

This time, look at the list of words below and decide what is the main idea of this group. (**Hint:** The main idea is not mentioned!)

What is the main idea that connects these things?

(A) candles

(B) games

(C) ice cream

(D) cake

(E) gifts

(F) guests

What do you think? _____

Think of a main idea that would include all of these things. You might come to the conclusion that the answer is a *birthday party*. In this case, you have to draw your own conclusion. In other words, you have to make a good guess at what the main idea is, even though it does not appear in words.

Sometimes the main idea of a paragraph is given in words directly—as in the solar system example above—but sometimes the main idea is only suggested, as in the birthday party example.

Try and Discuss *(cont.)*

Now take a look at an actual paragraph. Then decide what the main idea is.

Welcome Pool Members!

Welcome to the Millertown pool, created by the parks and recreation department for all residents of Millertown. Please keep in mind that many people use the pool in the summer and that rules must be followed. First, running, pushing, or shoving is never allowed. Walk slowly. Second, do not jump from the side of the pool. You might land on someone and hurt the person. Use the diving board for jumping instead. Third, it is good to have fun in the pool, but no rough play is permitted. If the lifeguard sees dangerous behavior, the swimmers will be told to stop immediately. Enjoy yourself while you're here—Millertown pool is for everyone!

The main idea of this paragraph is

   (A) summer.

   (B) swimming.

   (C) pool safety.

   (D) having fun.

Fill in the correct circle.

Ⓐ   Ⓑ   Ⓒ   Ⓓ

This paragraph is an example of one of those times when you must both recognize important details or clues and draw conclusions on your own.

Eliminate choices by looking for details. For example, you might think that (A) "summer" is correct because, after all, people go to a pool in the summer. But look closely. How many details are about summer in the paragraph? The summer months are not mentioned; the temperature in the summertime is not mentioned. There are no details about summer.

How about choice (B) "swimming"? The paragraph is all about swimming or, at least, using the pool. But in fact, there are no details about how to swim or when to swim. Most of the details—"walk slowly" and "no rough play"—are about safety at the pool. So (C) "pool safety" is the correct answer. What about (D) "having fun"? Draw your own conclusion; see how many details about having fun you can find in the paragraph.

Tips That Help

Remember the following tips:

- The main idea in a paragraph covers all the other ideas in the paragraph or passage.
- Sometimes you must draw your own conclusion. Look for details that support your good guess about what the main idea is.

 Now try the practice tests. Follow the test directions and solve the sample problems to be sure you understand what to do on each test.

Directions: Read each passage, and answer the questions that follow.

> As an author, Judy Blume mined her childhood for the concerns and problems faced by many of her characters. As a child, she said, she was like Sheila in Otherwise Known as Sheila the Great (1972): afraid of thunderstorms, attics, and learning to swim. At the age of nine, she and her brother moved to Florida for two years for her brother's health. This period of her life influenced Starring Sally J. Freedman as Herself (1977), which Blume calls her most autobiographical book. Sally fears that her forty-two-year-old father will die because two of her uncles died at that age. Blume also had two uncles who had died young. Death evidently weighed on her mind for other reasons, too. She stated in the introduction to the British edition of *Sally* that she was just seven years old when World War II ended. She added that the war had affected her so much, it was very difficult to think of anything else. She knew that Adolf Hitler was a dangerous man because he wanted to destroy all the Jews in the world. And she was a Jew.

1. Which of the following is NOT true?
   (A) Judy Blume uses problems from her own childhood in her books.
   (B) Blume's family moved to Florida to escape Adolf Hitler during World War II.
   (C) *Starring Sally J. Freedman as Herself* is mainly about Blume herself.
   (D) Both the character Sally and Judy Blume had uncles who died young.

> Although most people are aware that girls' athletics offer the same physical benefit as boys' athletics—overall fitness—recent studies have shown that girls' participation in sports carries some unforseen benefits, too. First, girls who participate in sports report having fewer problems with depression and feeling higher self-esteem than those who don't participate. Perhaps this partly accounts for why female athletes graduate at a higher rate, 69 percent, compared to 51 percent of girls who are not in sports. The outlook for even more young women participating in sports seems likely, especially since a survey of parents found that 83 percent believe that girls' athletic programs are as important as boys.

2. Which of the following is NOT true?
   (F) Female athletes get mental as well as physical benefits from sports.
   (G) Most parents think girls' sports are as important as boys'.
   (H) Being in sports, though, interferes with girls graduating.
   (J) More girls will probably be participating in sports in the future.

GO →

Directions: Read each passage, and answer the questions that follow.

Samuel Langhorne Clemens (Mark Twain) was born on November 30, 1835, in Florida, a log village on the Missouri frontier. His parents had come there from the hills of Tennessee. When he was four, the family moved again to Hannibal, a larger town of five hundred people on the Mississippi River. His father, a merchant and trader, died when Clemens was twelve. His mother was unable to make him attend school regularly, so she arranged to have him be an apprentice to local printers, beginning his lifetime association with newspaper work, travel writing, and publishing. As a teenager, Clemens worked in his brother Orion's printing shop, a business that designed and set in type posters, newspapers, and notices. Using the name W. Spaminodas Adrastas Blab, Clemens wrote and published his first few humorous columns for a newspaper that came through his brother's shop. Clemens now had a trade that would allow him to satisfy an urge to travel.

---

3. Which of the following is NOT true?
   (A) Clemens' mother had trouble with him after his father died.
   (B) Clemens began writing stories as a teenager.
   (C) Clemens' mother's decision to make him go to work was a wise choice.
   (D) Clemens worked for a printer named W. Spaminodas Adrastas Blab.

During a few days of unusually warm weather in 1993, hikers in the Tyrolean Alps—a mountain range that borders Italy and Austria—came upon a startling sight. Trapped in the melting ice and snow was the body of a man. Police were summoned to the scene, but soon the authorities realized that this was not a case of a recent hiker who had lost his way. "The Iceman," as newspapers called him, is the oldest and best-preserved human body ever found. Careful examination by anthropologists showed that the wind and cold had dried the flesh like a mummy's. He had been a man in mid-life, about 5' 3" tall, and weighing 110 pounds. His dark hair and beard were cut short. But how long ago had he journeyed into the Alps? Radiocarbon tests conducted on his body and tools—including the grains of grassland pollen found on his wool clothing—indicated that the Iceman had lived before Mohammed, Christ, or Buddha. He was at least 5,000 years old!

---

4. Which of the following is TRUE?
   (F) The Iceman died in 1993.
   (G) For some reason, the Iceman was taking a mummy into the Alps.
   (H) Hikers lost their way and froze to death.
   (J) At first, no one realized how old the Iceman's body was.

GO →

Directions: An *inference* is a conclusion you draw on your own. For example, if you tried to turn on a TV and nothing happened, you would make the inference that the TV isn't working.

Read the following passages and choose the statement you think is a correct inference.

"Arthur, are you down there?" I yelled down the basement stairs.

I felt like an old fishwife screeching like that, but he was probably sitting at his workbench lost in thought on another ship model. And once Art gets going on assembling one of his super-detailed battleships, or PT boats, or man o'wars—whatever age of sailing he's currently wild about—well, the real world just kind of slips over the edge of the world like a remote shore disappearing from sight.

"Anyone below?" I tried loudly.

No answer, just a polite cough.

I trudged down a couple of steps to where I could see into the corner of the basement. Sure enough, there he was—perched on his stool, wearing headphones, and humming to himself. The spotlight cast by his special high-intensity lamp fell on a three-mast wooden ship, receiving his careful attention like a patient on an operating table.

I walked up behind him, lifted one of his earphones and said, "Ahoy, Admiral Findley!"

He jumped. "For heaven's sake, Barbara, don't do that! You could've done damage to my main mast here!" He pointed sternly to a slender piece of wood in the center of the model, which looked to me like a varnished chopstick trailing threads.

5. (A) Two boys belong to a model-building club.
   (B) A wife is trying to get her husband's attention.
   (C) Two people are sailing on a ship.
   (D) A nurse needs a doctor's help immediately.

On the morning the ambulance came to get Delbert Hudson, there was a big, big crowd.

His mother was there, worried and upset—trying to push her way to the front so she could see. And when she did, she screamed and fell over, her hands going up like someone overcome by the spirit. Tony Albright—the Hudson's neighbor—caught her in his arms. April and the baby were hugging each other and crying scared like there'd been a loud clap of thunder suddenly. And even Mrs. Nixon, who was looking out her window just as Delbert fell to the ground, managed to get down her steps in time to see.

On that morning, there were all kinds of people in the street, looking down at the boy in the jacket with blood on it.

6. (F) A crowd is cheering someone on.
   (G) An athlete has been injured.
   (H) A boy has been injured in the street.
   (J) A thunderstorm is upsetting children in a neighborhood.

GO →

"You see 'im?" Everett says. "The old oak directly across."

Everett Olsen is lying next me on the hill leading up to Wilkin's abandoned pasture. The grass—dry as straw from weeks of Indian summer in Pennsylvania—prickles our skin as we face one another, flushed and panting.

Lying between us and longer than either of us by a several inches is Ev's new squirrel rifle.

Ev flicks his eyes in the direction of the pasture indicating I should have a look-see myself. I crawl to the tip of the hill, take off my cap so as not to present a better target, and pop up my head. The overgrown grasses are riffling slightly in the late afternoon breeze. I study the scene carefully, and then prop myself on my elbow carelessly and gaze down at my best friend.

"Heck fire, there's nothin'," I say, plucking a stalk of grass to chew on.

He snorts. "You see a puff of smoke from over there and it'll be the last thing you ever see."

I duck down and slide back next to him.

He looks at me fiercely. "It's a Johnny Reb, Warren—I seen him yesterday! He must've got separated from his unit over t'Gettysburg!" In frustration, he clutches the shoulder of my jacket and hauls me up to where I can see again. "Now look directly ahead—the big oak in the middle, and halfway up," he says, pointing. "Like a bear."

The wind shivers the big oak, the one he's talking about. Then suddenly, I can make-out—perched in the center of its branches—a figure, his back against the giant trunk and astride one of the thickest limbs, sighting over the barrel of a rifle at us.

"Jeez-o pete—a sniper," I whisper reverently and scuttle backwards.

7. (A) Two boys have found a Confederate soldier hiding in a tree.
   (B) A farmer is guarding his field against trespassers.
   (C) Two boys are pretending they're hunting.
   (D) Two soldiers are lost.

I didn't have a very interesting life—or even a very interesting job, for that matter. If I had, it might have been some comfort in coping with my loneliness.

I worked for a large advertising firm in Chicago, right on the Magnificent Mile overlooking the river. When I would tell people that, they'd say, "What a wonderful job for a young woman, how exciting!" But the truth is, the key to advertising is making people think they want something—making them believe they have to have it to be happy. And as the years passed, I began to realize the irony of selling dreams when my own dreams had gone unfilled.

8. (F) The speaker is very proud of her job.
   (G) The speaker is upset that the company she works for doesn't know about her dreams.
   (H) The speaker's job is to sell her dreams to others.
   (J) The speaker feels her life isn't working out.

STOP

Directions: Read the passage below, and answer the questions.

Book Review

(*Alice Rose & Sam* by Kathryn Lasky. Hyperion, New York. 252 pages.)

Before Mark Twain was the spinner of tall tales, travelogues, boys' stories, and memoirs of life on the Mississippi, he was a wandering typesetter, riverboat pilot, Confederate deserter, failed prospector, and hard-drinking newspaperman. In *Alice Rose & Sam*, Kathryn Lasky provides a fictionalized glimpse of Twain's humbler days as Sam Clemens in Virginia City, Nevada, where he makes up pretend news events for the *Territorial Enterprise* newspaper.

Lasky overlaps Clemens' early life with the unhappy existence of Alice Rose Tucker, a twelve-year-old with a vivid imagination who is trying to live out her childhood in Virginia City, a place that is sad, comical, and dangerous. Her mother and siblings have all died: "There were little Tucker babies planted all over the plains and prairies and deserts of the West." Her father is a dreamer who is one of the "boys" over at the newspaper. Alice Rose earns money as a dressmaker for the fancy ladies of the saloons. She and Clemens become allies when they witness the shooting of a man in an alley. Circumstances suggest a conspiracy between Confederate sympathizers and a weird Christian outfit called the Society of Seven.

Lasky tries hard to weave a story out of the facts. The result, however, is a shambling, loose-jointed tale bothered by incomplete characterizations—Clemens in particular comes off as a simpleton—and poorly conceived subplots. A quest by Alice Rose to find a little Chinese boy, for example, peters out in Chinatown with no explanation. On the other hand, the evilness of the Society of Seven depends so much on political and religious values of the day that teenage readers will probably skip over this stuff completely. *Alice Rose & Sam* is somewhere between a pretend biography, an adventure story, and a how-to book on silver mining in the Old West, but the story falls between the cracks.

1. The reviewer of *Alice Rose & Sam* admires the book.
   - (A) True
   - (B) False

2. *Alice Rose & Sam* is a biography of Mark Twain as a young man.
   - (A) True
   - (B) False

3. Alice Rose lives with her mother and brothers in Virginia City, Nevada.
   - (A) True
   - (B) False

4. Alice Rose does not enjoy her life in Virginia City.
   - (A) True
   - (B) False

5. Alice Rose and Sam Clemens are Confederates who join a weird Christian society.
   - (A) True
   - (B) False

6. One of the best parts of the book is how Alice Rose tracks down a lost boy in Chinatown.
   - (A) True
   - (B) False

GO →

Directions: Read the verse below, and fill in the circle of the correct response for each question.

Get a Transfer*

If you are on the Gloomy Line,
Get a transfer.
If you're inclined to fret and pine,
Get a transfer.
Get off the track of doubt and gloom,
Get on the Sunshine Track—there's room—
Get a transfer.

If you're on the Worry Train
Get a transfer.
You must not stay there and complain,
Get a transfer.
The Cheerful Cars are passing through,
And there's lots of room for you—
Get a transfer.

If you're on the Grouchy Track,
Get a transfer.
Just take a Happy Special back,
Get a transfer.
Jump on the train and pull the rope,
That lands you at the station Hope—
Get a transfer.
—Author Unknown

*Get a transfer means "change trains."

7. Each set of seven lines is called a
   (A) chorus.
   (B) stanza.
   (C) verse.
   (D) paragraph.

8. The accented and unaccented syllables in each line is called
   (F) rhythm.
   (G) beats.
   (H) meter.
   (J) stress.

9. The rhyme scheme of "Get a Transfer" is
   (A) abcdefg.
   (B) ababccb.
   (C) abacdde.
   (D) aabbccd.

10. The phrase "Get a transfer" is called a
    (F) chorus.
    (G) refrain.
    (H) repeat.
    (J) rondo.

11. This piece of verse is about
    (A) being on the right train.
    (B) getting somewhere fast.
    (C) learning how to get around.
    (D) changing your attitude.

12. Using a train to express an idea is
    (F) an image.
    (G) an idea.
    (H) a metaphor.
    (J) a goal.

➤ **STOP** ◄

Directions: Read the plot summary of the book, *Whirligig*, by Paul Fleischman. Then answer the questions following the passage.

Plot Summary

(*Whirligig* by Paul Fleischman. Henry Holt & Co., Inc. 160 pages.)

Brent Bishop wants to be popular. He launches his junior year as a newcomer in a pricey, private school near Chicago like a sniper aiming at a target. He makes sure he has the right clothes. He wears his earring in the correct ear, and he eagerly accepts an invitation to a lawn party where the popular kids of the school will be.

Arriving at the party, however, he is embarrassed. There is a dress code, and the host of the party, looking at Brent's Chicago Bulls T-shirt mutters, "Points off." The second embarrassment is an outright public humiliation by a girl he is attracted to. "Stop hanging all over me!" she screams in front of Brent's stunned and amused classmates. He storms out of the party and roars down the expressway. Then, in an act that shows his extreme immaturity and selfishness, Brent shuts his eyes and lets go of the wheel of his speeding car.

He survives a crash, but kills the driver of another car, Lea, a girl his own age. Once so eager to be accepted, Brent has made himself an outcast in society. A judge sentences Brent to probation and counseling. However, Brent and his parents are not prepared for the judge's third order: that Brent meet Lea's mother.

The meeting turns out not to be what Brent expected. Lea's mother does not want revenge. She makes an unusual request instead. She wants Brent to build whirligigs—wind-driven sculptures—on the four corners of the United States to commemorate Lea's spirit. Brent seizes the chance to do something, anything to make up for what he has done and accepts the mission.

The author describes Brent's experiences as he wanders on Greyhound buses across America. The combination of being by himself, along with the concentration it takes to build the whirligigs (He carries a picture of Lea and makes the last whirligig look like her.) changes him completely. He discovers that real life is much deeper, more important, and more valuable than he knew. Special chapters between Brent's story show how the finished whirligigs give hope, enjoyment, or insight to people who come upon them long after he has finished them and left. By the story's end, Brent is close to where he can forgive himself in this highly readable novel.

GO →

1. The *conflict* in this novel is
   (A) Brent versus the justice system.
   (B) Brent versus Lea's mother.
   (C) Brent versus himself.
   (D) Brent versus nature.

2. The *setting* in this novel is
   (F) now.
   (G) the party and the courtroom.
   (H) Chicago and parts of the United States.
   (J) in Brent's mind.

3. A *symbol* in the novel is
   (A) the judge.
   (B) the whirligigs.
   (C) Brent.
   (D) the car crash.

4. The *crisis* in the novel is
   (F) the party.
   (G) meeting Lea's mother.
   (H) the car crash.
   (J) the trip on the Greyhound buses.

5. Being selfish is part of Brent's
   (A) history.
   (B) upbringing.
   (C) world.
   (D) character.

6. A *theme* for this novel might be
   (F) the world is unfair.
   (G) thinking about other people, not just yourself, makes life richer.
   (H) violent people get what they deserve.
   (J) art can change your outlook.

GO →

Directions: Read the essay below, and choose the best answer for each question. Look for the main idea in each paragraph. (*Hint:* The main idea is not always the first sentence.)

Camping with a Tent

by Johnny Phong

I. (A) <u>Every year my family takes off a week or two during the summer for a vacation, so we have a lot of experiences about how to have a great vacation camping outdoors.</u> (B) <u>It is actually not only my family; thousands of people throughout the United States also choose to spend their vacations camping in the great outdoors.</u> (C) <u>Depending on an individual's sense of adventure, there are various types of camping to choose from, including log cabin camping, recreational vehicle camping, and tent camping.</u> (D) <u>Of these, tent camping involves roughing it the most, and with proper planning the experience can be gratifying.</u> However, even with the best planning, tent camping can be an extremely frustrating experience due to uncontrolled factors such as bad weather, wildlife encounters, and equipment failures.

II. Nothing can dampen the excited anticipation of camping more than a dark, rainy day. Even the most adventurous campers can lose some of their enthusiasm on the drive to the campsite if the skies are dreary and damp. (F) <u>After reaching their destination, campers must then "set up camp" in the downpour.</u> This includes keeping the inside of the tent dry and free from mud, getting the sleeping bags situated dryly, and protecting food from the downpour. (G) <u>If the sleeping bags happen to get wet, the cold also becomes a major factor.</u> A sleeping bag usually provides warmth on a camping trip; a wet sleeping bag provides none. Combining wind with rain can cause frigid temperatures, causing any outside activities to be delayed. (H) <u>Even inside the tent problems may arise due to heavy winds.</u> More than a few campers have had their tents blown down because of the wind, which once again begins the frustrating task of "setting up camp" in the downpour. (J) <u>It is wise to check the weather forecast before embarking on camping trips.</u> Mother nature is often unpredictable and there is no guarantee bad weather will be avoided.

III. (A) <u>Another problem likely to be faced during a camping trip is run-ins with wildlife, which can range from mildly annoying to dangerous.</u> Minor inconveniences include mosquitoes and ants. The swarming of mosquitoes can literally drive annoyed campers indoors. If an effective repellent is not used, the camper can spend an interminable night scratching, which will only worsen the itch. (B) <u>Ants do not usually attack campers, but keeping them out of the food can be quite an inconvenience.</u> Extreme care must be taken not to leave food out before or after meals. If food is stored inside the tent, the tent must never be left open. In addition to swarming the food, ants inside a tent can crawl into sleeping bags and clothing. (C) <u>Although these insects cause minor discomfort, some wildlife encounters are potentially dangerous.</u> There are many poisonous snakes in the United States, such as the water moccasin and the diamond-back rattlesnake. (D) <u>When hiking in the woods, the camper must be careful where he steps.</u> Also, the tent must never be left open. Snakes, searching for either shade from the sun or shelter from the rain, can enter a tent. An encounter between an unwary camper and a surprised snake can prove to be fatal. Run-ins can range from unpleasant to dangerous, but the camper must realize that they are sometimes inevitable.

GO →

Camping with a Tent *(cont.)*

IV. (F) <u>Perhaps the least serious camping troubles are equipment failures; these troubles often plague families camping for the first time.</u> They arrive at the campsite at night and haphazardly set up their nine-person tent. They then settle down for a peaceful night's rest. (G) <u>Sometime during the night the family is awakened by a huge crash.</u> The tent has fallen down. Sleepily, they awake and proceed to set up the tent in the rain. In the morning, everyone emerges from the tent, except for two. Their sleeping bag zippers have gotten caught. Finally, after fifteen minutes of struggling, they free themselves, only to realize another problem. Each of the family members' sleeping bags has been touching the sides of the tent. A tent is only waterproof if the sides are not touched. Their sleeping bags and clothing are all drenched. (H) <u>Totally disillusioned with their vacation, the frustrated family packs up immediately and drives home.</u> (J) <u>Equipment failures may not seem very serious, but after campers encounter bad weather and annoying pests or wild animals, these failures can end any remaining hope for a peaceful vacation.</u>

V. (A) <u>These three types of camping troubles can strike campers almost anywhere.</u> (B) <u>Until some brilliant scientist invents a weather machine to control bad weather or a kind of wildlife repellent, unlucky campers will continue to shake their fists in frustration.</u> (C) <u>And, more than likely, equipment will continue to malfunction.</u> (D) <u>Even so, the rewards of camping are plentiful, and it continues to be a favorite pastime of people all across the United States.</u>

7. The main idea in paragraph I is
(A) sentence A.
(B) sentence B.
(C) sentence C.
(D) sentence D.

8. The main idea in paragraph II is
(F) sentence F.
(G) sentence G.
(H) sentence H.
(J) sentence J.

9. The main idea in paragraph III is
(A) sentence A.
(B) sentence B.
(C) sentence C.
(D) sentence D.

10. The main idea in paragraph IV is
(F) sentence F.
(G) sentence G.
(H) sentence H.
(J) sentence J.

11. The main idea in paragraph V is
(A) sentence A.
(B) sentence B.
(C) sentence C.
(D) sentence D.

➤ STOP ≺

Directions: Choose the correct part of speech for each underlined word or words. Here are vocabulary meanings for the following Spanish words:

- *Abuela*: Grandmother
- *Sopa de fideo*: noodle soup
- *Sopa de fideo con pollo*: chicken soup with noodles
- *tortilla*: flat bread

Excerpt from *Abuela Goes*

by Guadalupe Shields

Abuela Lupe sits down with her <u>morning</u> cup <u>of coffee</u> to plan her day. Today is
                              1   2

<u>Thursday</u>, the day she always goes shopping. First, she <u>thinks</u> about something <u>special</u> that she
3   4   5

might prepare for dinner tonight because her son, Roberto, <u>is</u> coming to visit. "*Sopa de fideo*,"
                                    6

she thinks. "<u>Roberto</u> loves my *sopa de fideo con pollo* with *tortillas*, <u>refried</u> beans, and <u>rice</u>."
           7   8   9

Abuela Lupe checks her pantry <u>and</u> sees that she is going to need *fideo*, tomatoes, and
                               10

those <u>wonderful</u> cookies Roberto likes to have with his coffee <u>after dinner.</u>
        11   12

Abuela Lupe also has to buy a few <u>groceries</u> for her sister, Sara. Sara is a <u>babysitter</u> for
                                13   14

her daughter Isabel's twin boys, <u>Jaime and Isidro</u>, while Isabel is in the hospital with a new
                                  15

baby girl. <u>By the time Sara gets home</u>, it will be dark, and the grocery store <u>will be closed</u>. So
              16   17

Sara has asked *Abuela* Lupe to pick up a <u>few</u> things for her: a package of corn *tortillas*, a jar of
                                18

horseradish, two cans of black olives, and a <u>ten-pound</u> bag of apples. Sara <u>wants to bake an</u>
                                           19   20

<u>apple pie for Isabel and the baby's homecoming dinner.</u>
         20

GO →

1. (A) pronoun
   (B) adjective
   (C) article
   (D) adverb

2. (F) clause
   (G) prepositional phrase
   (H) noun
   (J) verb

3. (A) adjective
   (B) noun
   (C) proper noun
   (D) adverb

4. (F) verb
   (G) noun
   (H) adverb
   (J) adjective

5. (A) adverb
   (B) adjective
   (C) noun
   (D) verb

6. (F) linking verb
   (G) adverb
   (H) article
   (J) pronoun

7. (A) proper noun
   (B) noun
   (C) pronoun
   (D) both A & C

8. (F) verb
   (G) adverb
   (H) noun
   (J) adjective

9. (A) noun
   (B) pronoun
   (C) conjunction
   (D) adjective

10. (F) linking verb
    (G) conjunction
    (H) article
    (J) adjective

11. (A) verb
    (B) adjective
    (C) subject complement
    (D) appositive

12. (F) gerund
    (G) prepositional phrase
    (H) adjective
    (J) noun

13. (A) pronoun
    (B) direct object
    (C) preposition
    (D) indirect object

14. (F) subject complement
    (G) verb
    (H) adjective
    (J) pronoun

15. (A) proper nouns
    (B) appositives
    (C) pronouns
    (D) both A & B

16. (F) independent clause
    (G) dependent clause
    (H) simple subject
    (J) complete predicate

17. (A) verb
    (B) adverb
    (C) prepositional phrase
    (D) adjective

18. (F) noun
    (G) pronoun
    (H) adjective
    (J) adverb

19. (A) compound noun
    (B) plural noun
    (C) compound adjective
    (D) adjective-noun

20. (F) complete predicate
    (G) complete subject
    (H) complete verb
    (J) complete sentence

> **STOP** <

Language Arts: Writing Competencies (cont.)

Directions: Read the passage below. If the underlined item has a mistake, choose the correct answer. If there is no mistake, choose "no mistake."

(**Note:** The Spanish word, *abuela*, means grandmother.)

Sample

"Roberto, come in here <u>at once</u>"

        (A) at once.   (B) at once?   (C) at once!   (D) no mistake

---

Another Excerpt from *Abuela Goes*
by Guadalupe Shields

The telephone rings. <u>Its</u> *Abuela* Lupe's neighbor, Margaret, who lives two houses down

         1

and across the street. Margaret is home with a bad <u>cold Her</u> husband is out of town and

         2

Margaret is all alone. <u>"Hello Lupe?</u> It's me, Margaret. How are you? I still have (achoo!) that

      3

bad cold. Are you going shopping <u>today.</u> Can you stop by Johnson's Drugstore and pick up a

      4

couple of things for <u>me"?</u>

    5

"Oh, Margaret, I'm so sorry to hear that you are sick. Of course, I'll stop at the drugstore

for <u>you,"</u> says *Abuela* Lupe. <u>"what</u> do you need?" They talk a little more and then *Abuela* Lupe

  6   7

gets ready to go. The walk to the grocery store is eight blocks away. It's <u>late october</u> and there

                       8

is a chill in the air. She finds her purple fuzzy hat with the matching scarf that Roberto gave her

for her birthday last year. (She was born <u>April 20 1945.</u>) As she starts for the <u>door the</u>

           9   10

telephone rings again.

GO →

1.

    (A) Its'   (B) It's   (C) Its's   (D) no mistake

2.

    (F) cold, Her   (G) cold her   (H) cold. Her   (J) no mistake

3.

    (A) "Hello, Lupe?   (B) "Hello, Lupe?"   (C) "Hello, Lupe"?   (D) no mistake

4.

    (F) today!   (G) today,   (H) today?   (J) no mistake

5.

    (A) me? (no quotes)   (B) me?'   (C) me?"   (D) no mistake

6.

    (F) you",   (G) you."   (H) you, (no quotes)   (J) no mistake

7.

    (A) what (no quotes)   (B) "What   (C) What   (D) no mistake

8.

    (F) late October   (G) late, october   (H) late, October   (J) no mistake

9.

    (A) April 20/1945.   (B) April 20, 1945.   (C) april 20, 1945.   (D) no mistake

10.

    (F) door. The   (G) door, the   (H) door-the   (J) no mistake

GO →

Directions: Choose the letter of the word that is spelled INCORRECTLY. If all the words are spelled correctly, fill in the circle for "no mistake."

11.
 (A) adjourn
 (B) allegory
 (C) disapoint
 (D) no mistake

12.
 (F) easiness
 (G) gorey
 (H) character
 (J) no mistake

13.
 (A) motercycle
 (B) unachieved
 (C) visible
 (D) no mistake

14.
 (F) teammate
 (G) purchase
 (H) squeaker
 (J) no mistake

15.
 (A) aligator
 (B) kerchief
 (C) hierarchy
 (D) no mistake

16.
 (F) briefcase
 (G) hare
 (H) postpone
 (J) no mistake

17.
 (A) zodiac
 (B) uncurl
 (C) wieght
 (D) no mistake

18.
 (F) ivory
 (G) lunchon
 (H) spiteful
 (J) no mistake

19.
 (A) masthead
 (B) lamb
 (C) oasis
 (D) no mistake

20.
 (F) island
 (G) aisle
 (H) likewize
 (J) no mistake

21.
 (A) federal
 (B) halestone
 (C) paragraph
 (D) no mistake

➤ **STOP** ◄

Directions: The passage below, taken from a school report about mental health, has a number of errors in it. Look at the underlined word or words. Identify the kind of error. If there is no error, fill in the circle for "no error."

Sample

Most young people would rather suffer <u>then</u> admit they had a mental health problem.
   (A) spelling problem
   (B) capitalization problem
   (C) no error

School Mental Health Report

       A poll taken by the National <u>mental health</u> Association found that more than half of
                            1

<u>American</u> believe that embarrassment about mental illness prevents people from seeking
  2

treatment. Nineteen <u>million</u> Americans suffer from anxiety <u>disorders fewer</u> than one-third
                  3   4

receive <u>treatment Also</u>, according to the Children's Defense Fund, fewer than <u>one third</u> of
         5   6

children under the age of 18 with a serious <u>emotoinal disturbance receive</u> mental health
                                      7

services. Part of the problem is that <u>parents</u> fears about a child's mental health can drive some
                                8

parents into denial. Also, <u>young people is</u> sensitive about what classmates think. Many
                     9

<u>students rather</u> suffer <u>silent</u> than be singled out as '<u>weird.</u>" <u>So, rather than face teasing or</u>
    10   11   12   13

<u>criticism.</u> They will try to cope as best they can. This means <u>parents and school official</u>
  13   14

should be alert to warning signs that may point to a possible mental health problem.

GO →

1.
   - (A) spelling problem
   - (B) capitalization problem
   - (C) no error

2.
   - (F) capitalization problem
   - (G) plural problem
   - (H) no error

3.
   - (A) spelling problem
   - (B) capitalization problem
   - (C) no error

4.
   - (F) semi-colon problem
   - (G) plural problem
   - (H) no error

5.
   - (A) period problem
   - (B) comma problem
   - (C) no error

6.
   - (F) hyphen problem
   - (G) comma problem
   - (H) no error

7.
   - (A) spelling problem
   - (B) comma problem
   - (C) no error

8.
   - (F) apostrophe problem
   - (G) plural problem
   - (H) no error

9.
   - (A) comma problem
   - (B) subject-verb agreement problem
   - (C) no error

10.
   - (F) missing word problem
   - (G) apostrophe problem
   - (H) no error

11.
   - (A) spelling problem
   - (B) adverb problem
   - (C) no error

12.
   - (F) apostrophe problem
   - (G) quotation mark problem
   - (H) no error

13.
   - (A) fragment problem
   - (B) verb problem
   - (C) no error

14.
   - (F) apostrophe problem
   - (G) plural problem
   - (H) no error

➤ **STOP** ◄

Directions: Read the newspaper editorial below, then write a letter to the editor either agreeing or disagreeing with the writer's opinion. Your letter should be a persuasive essay that includes the following:

- introduction
- 3–5 paragraphs of 4–6 sentences each
- 2–3 reasons for agreeing or disagreeing with the editorial
- conclusion

Today's Tricksters Are Tomorrow's Hackers: Students Need Computer Ethics Now

The students in Mrs. Miller's seventh-grade class at Anywhere Middle School were excited about using computers as part of their regular instruction. The school board had provided each classroom with computers and phone line connections that would permit the students to connect with museums, colleges, and magazines—even other schools! Each student was assigned his or her own e-mail address for receiving private messages, too.

The kids were excited; so were their parents; so were the members of the school board.

And then, about a month after Mrs. Miller's class went online, the problems started. Arthur got angry at Meagan for some reason and erased her disk with all her original stories on it. Angela was supposed to be writing a report on the Civil War, so she copied an article from an electronic encyclopedia, pasted it into her report, added her name, and handed it in. Kyle sent Andrew an insulting e-mail message. He sent it to ten other kids, so Andrew would have their ridicule to deal with, too. Ellen played a trick on everyone else waiting to use the printer by setting it on 50 copies of an article she was reading, and then walked away. Tamika e-mailed fourth graders in England and lied by saying she was the teacher, Mrs. Miller.

All work on computers was suspended immediately. Someone on the school board remarked that maybe seventh graders aren't ready for networked computers in the classroom.

But they are! Seventh graders and students much younger know right from wrong. If you ask a child whether it's right to lie, he'll say no. But he may not understand that copying someone else's work from a Web site is wrong.

Ask him if you should ever grab someone's Walkman and break it. He'll say no again. But erasing a disk? Well, the disk still can be used, can't it? It is just that all the "stuff" on it is gone.

What children like Mrs. Miller's class need to learn, and schools in general are becoming aware of, is the importance of computer ethics. Computer ethics means recognizing and practicing right from wrong when using computers.

Computers, electronic communication, and online research are here to stay in school. And so are the opportunities to be dishonest in ways that leave no fingerprints, unfortunately.

GO →

Today's Tricksters Are Tomorrow's Hackers: Students Need Computer Ethics Now *(cont.)*

Already, many students are under the impression that information is free, that if it can be copied, it should be. Most students would never steal a computer game from a store, but they make copies of them. Most would never break into a place they don't belong, but guessing passwords and entering forbidden areas has taken on flavor of a sport.

Moreover, many popular movies make unethical actions seem heroic. Who can resist the appeal of sympathetic characters played by movie idols stealing American secrets to clear their names? It's just the government—they're nobody! It's not much of a stretch for a child to assume that anyone on the other end of an electronic communication is really nobody, either. The seventh-grade trickster who breaks into the teacher's grade book today and changes everyone's grades could be the code breaker of tomorrow who gets into the files of a major bank and moves people's savings around.

Right now, we need to teach kids right from wrong about computers and about using the information highway appropriately.

➤ STOP ◄

Introduction

To perform your best on the mathematics section of a standardized test, you need not know the right answer every time. But you do need to use two important strategies that will improve your score: *estimating* and *recognizing a reasonable answer*.

Here's the Idea

Estimating is a way of getting close to a right answer by rounding. When you round numbers in a problem, you will get an answer that is close to the right answer.

Recognizing a reasonable answer means deciding that an answer choice is probably right, based on what you already know about numbers and problems. You can drop some answer choices right away because they are not reasonable.

However, before we look at these two skills, below are some tips that apply to taking any test, whether it is in language arts, mathematics, science, social studies, fine arts, or computers and technology. These tips will be repeated because they are important!

Test-Taking Tips

- **Read directions carefully before marking any test questions,** even though you have done that kind of test before. You may think you already know what the directions say, but don't ignore them—read them over. If you don't understand the directions, raise your hand and ask for help. Although your teacher must read the directions exactly as they are written, the teacher can make sure you understand what the directions mean.

- **Follow instructions.** Pay close attention to the sample exercises. They will help you understand what the items on the test will be like and how to mark your answer sheet properly.

- **Read the entire question and all the answer choices.** Do not stop reading when you have found a correct answer. Choices D or E may read "B and D" or "all of the above" or "none of the above." On some tests, two answers are both correct. You need to read all the answer choices before marking your answer.

- **And remember—taking a test is not a race!** There are no prizes for finishing first. Use all of the time provided for the test. If you have time left over, check your answers.

Try and Discuss

Now let's discuss those two skills for mathematics tests—*estimating* and *recognizing a reasonable answer*. When you estimate, you use round numbers to come close to the correct answer without even working the problem through. Use these two rules for rounding:

- Round <u>up</u> for numbers five and greater than five.
- Round <u>down</u> for numbers less than five.

Immigrants to the United States, 1976–1986

Country of Origin	Approximate Numbers
Mexico	720,000
Vietnam	425,000
Philippines	379,000
Korea	363,000

SOURCE: Foner, Eric and John A. Garrity, eds. *The Reader's Companion to American History* (Boston: Houghton Mifflin, 1991) 538.

How many fewer immigrants came from Vietnam than Mexico?

(A) 220,250 (B) 120,250

(C) 295,000 (D) 350,000

Fill in the correct circle.

Ⓐ Ⓑ Ⓒ Ⓓ

If you round down 720,000 to 700,000 and round down 425,000 to 400,000 you can do the subtraction in your head: 300,000. Which answer comes closest? The answer is (C) 295,000. Estimating works well when you don't know the answer, or you're trying to go faster on a test because time is short.

Now what about recognizing a reasonable answer? Reasonable means "likely based on careful thinking." For instance, if you saw this problem:

200
x .4

(F) 800 (H) 80

(G) 60 (J) 20

Fill in the correct circle.

Ⓕ Ⓖ Ⓗ Ⓙ

You would know that (F) 800 is clearly not a reasonable answer. Two hundred is being multiplied by a decimal. (G) 60 is far less than half of 200, and 200 is being multiplied by .4 not .5. And (J) 20 is 10 percent of 200. You know these things already. Therefore, the answer is (H) 80.

Recognizing a reasonable answer is a powerful strategy when you want to eliminate answers. In other words, you can drop some answer choices immediately because they are not reasonable. Don't bother with answer choices that are clearly wrong because they are unreasonable. This improves your chances of choosing the correct answer, even if you have difficulty doing the problem.

Tips That Help

Remember the following:

- Use *estimating* to come close to the correct answer.
- Learn to *recognize a reasonable answer* so you can eliminate choices that are clearly wrong.

Now try the practice tests, listening to your teacher's directions.

Mathematics: Rational and Real Numbers

Directions: Read each question and choose the correct answer.

Write each number in scientific notation.

1. 3,400,000
   - (A) 34×10^6
   - (C) $.34 \times 10^6$
   - (B) 3.4×10^6
   - (D) 34×1000

2. 102,000
   - (F) 1.02×10^5
   - (G) 10.2×10^6
   - (H) 102×10^5
   - (J) $102 \times 10 \times 3$

3. 7,500
   - (A) 75×10^3
   - (B) 7.05×10^3
   - (C) 7.5×10^3
   - (D) $.75 \times 10^3$

Write each number in standard form.

4. 8.3×10^5
   - (F) 83,000
   - (H) 8,300
   - (G) 830
   - (J) 830,000

5. 2.25×10^3
   - (A) 2,250
   - (C) 225,000
   - (B) 22,500
   - (D) 225

What would be the next three terms?

6. 0.2, 0.4, 0.8, 1.6
   - (F) 46, 74, 120
   - (G) 3.2, 6.4, 12.8
   - (H) 1, 1.2, 1.4
   - (J) -19, -27, -35

7. What percent of 25 is 21?
   - (A) 80%
   - (B) 84%
   - (C) 82%
   - (D) 840%

8. What is 225% of 48?
   - (F) 70
   - (H) 108
   - (G) 72
   - (J) 96

9. Find 65% of 320
   - (A) 192
   - (B) 160
   - (C) 224
   - (D) 208

10. The sale price of a belt is $18. This is 80% of the original price. Find the original price.
    - (F) $2.25
    - (H) $225
    - (G) $22.50
    - (J) $20

11. The average daily attendance at James Hart Junior High is 92% of the school's enrollment. The average attendance is 422. What is the school's enrollment?
    - (A) 569 students
    - (B) 459 students
    - (C) 514 students
    - (D) 505 students

Solve for *y*.

12. 18 is 20% of *y*
    - (F) 9
    - (H) 900
    - (G) 90
    - (J) 38

13. 2% of *y* is 3
    - (A) 150
    - (C) 125
    - (B) 30
    - (D) 15

14. 140% of *y* is 210
    - (F) 30
    - (G) 125
    - (H) 150
    - (J) 15

> **STOP** <

Mathematics: Rational and Real Numbers *(cont.)*

Directions: Look at the factorization problems below. Fill in the circle for the correct answers to each problem.

1. Use prime factorization to find the least common multiple of 72 and 24.

   (A) 24   (C) 72

   (B) 216   (D) 36

2. Find the smallest number whose factors include 7, 2, and 4.

   (F) 13   (H) 28

   (G) 14   (J) 30

3. Find the smallest number whose factors include 11, 7, and 121.

   (A) 847   (C) 77

   (B) 139   (D) 1338

4. Find the greatest common factor of 24 and 2.

   (F) 1   (H) 3

   (G) 4   (J) 2

5. For Halloween, Spencer got 18 candy bars, 12 gumballs, and 36 chocolate drops. He wants to divide it all into groups so that each group has an equal number of candy bars, an equal number of gumballs, and an equal number of chocolate drops. What is the maximum number of groups he can make?

   (A) 2   (C) 12

   (B) 6   (D) 3

6. Find the greatest common factor of 36 and 6.

   (F) 3   (H) 12

   (G) 6   (J) 9

7. Mrs. Mikes, who runs the James Hart School store, has 28 tablets of paper, 98 erasers, and 196 pencils. She wants to divide the supplies into groups so that each group has an equal number of tablets, an equal number of erasers, and an equal number of pencils. What is the maximum number of groups she can make?

   (A) 7   (C) 28

   (B) 2   (D) 14

8. Find the smallest number whose factors include 2, 11, and 121.

   (F) 22   (H) 242

   (G) 253   (J) 134

9. Use prime factorization to find the least common multiple of 48 and 24.

   (A) 24   (C) 48

   (B) 96   (D) 16

10. Eli is trying to organize his toolbox. He has 50 bolts, 20 nuts, and 100 washers. He wants to divide it all into groups so that each group has an equal number of bolts, an equal number of nuts, and an equal number of washers. What is the maximum number of groups he can make?

    (F) 2   (H) 5

    (G) 10   (J) 20

11. Use prime factorization to find the least common multiple of 75 and 45.

    (A) 75   (C) 1125

    (B) 225   (D) 15

12. Find the smallest number whose factors include 7, 2, and 49.

    (F) 345   (H) 58

    (G) 14   (J) 98

➤ **STOP** ◄

Directions: Look at the fraction problems below. Fill in the circle for the correct answers to each problem.

1. Which two fractions are equivalent to 5/9?

   (A) 10/27, 15/18

   (B) 10/18, 25/81

   (C) 10/18, 15/27

   (D) 25/81, 15/27

2. What is the ratio of stars (*) to number signs (#)?

   ##*##*##*##*##

   (F) 4:5   (H) 9:5

   (G) 5:9   (J) 4:9

3. Which three fractions are equivalent to 1/3?

   (A) 3/12, 4/12, 3/9

   (B) 4/12, 2/6, 3/9

   (C) 2/6, 3/9, 9/12

   (D) 3/12, 3/6, 3/9

4. In a sack of birdseed, the ratio of sunflower seeds to corn kernels is 250 to 1,000. Write the ratio as a fraction in its simplest form.

   (F) 1/4

   (G) 1/8

   (H) 250/1,000

   (J) 1/2

5. Write 18/21 in its simplest form.

   (A) 7/6   (C) 3

   (B) 6/7   (D) 18

6. Write 80/90 in its simplest form.

   (F) 80   (H) 9/8

   (G) 8/9   (J) 10

7. Write 10/12 in its simplest form.

   (A) 6/5   (C) 5/6

   (B) 2   (D) 10

8. Solve the proportions. 4/9 = ?/27

   (F) 12   (H) 29

   (G) 24   (J) 8

9. Write 41/6 as a mixed number.

   (A) 6 5/6   (C) 7 5/6

   (B) 41 1/6   (D) 1 35/6

10. Charlie sold 36 tickets to the Thanksgiving Day dinner for the Lions Club. Dustin sold 30. What is the ratio of the number of tickets Charlie sold to the number of tickets Dustin sold?

    (F) 5/6   (H) 11/5

    (G) 6/5   (J) 5/11

11. Which group of fractions is equivalent to 1/10?

    (A) 1/100, 3/30

    (B) 2/20, 1/100

    (C) 2/30, 3/20

    (D) 2/20, 3/30

12. Find the common denominator of 3/6 and 2/7

    (F) 7   (H) 13

    (G) 3   (J) 42

13. Find the least common denominator of 5/7 and 5/56.

    (A) 224   (C) 28

    (B) 56   (D) 112

14. Find the least common denominator of 3/4 and 1/2.

    (F) 2   (H) 4

    (G) 1   (J) 3

➤ **STOP** ◄

Directions: Read each questions and choose the correct answer.

Classify each triangle by its angles.

1.

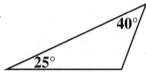

2.

3.

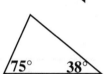

(A) obtuse

(B) right

(C) acute

(D) none of these

Match each description with its picture.

4. angle bisector

5. vertical angles

6. complementary angles

7. nonadjacent angles

(F)

(G)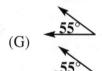

(H)

(J)

---

8. An angle is made up of two _____ with a common endpoint.

    (A) arcs   (B) angles   (C) intersections   (D) rays

---

9. The number of square units inside a figure is the

    (F) total.   (G) area.   (H) sum.   (J) cubic feet.

---

10. _____ is the distance around a circle.

    (A) radius   (B) diameter   (C) 3.14   (D) circumference

---

11. A (n) _____ triangle is a triangle with three congruent sides.

    (F) right   (G) pyramid   (H) equilateral   (J) obtuse

---

12. _____ is the distance around a figure.

    (A) perimeter   (B) area   (C) square root   (D) radii

➤ STOP ◄

Mathematics: Pre-Algebra

Directions: Evaluate each expression when $x = -8$, $y = 2$, and $z = 4$.

1. xy
   - (A) 16
   - (B) –16
   - (C) 6
   - (D) –6

2. yz
   - (F) 8
   - (G) 32
   - (H) –8
   - (J) 16

3. xz
   - (A) 32
   - (B) –32
   - (C) 16
   - (D) 26

4. xyz
   - (F) –64
   - (G) 64
   - (H) 14
   - (J) 28

5. x/y
   - (A) 4
   - (B) 8
   - (C) –4
   - (D) 12

6. A(n) _____ is a statement that two numbers or quantities are equal.
   - (F) solution
   - (G) equation
   - (H) problem
   - (J) answer

7. On a coordinate plane, the vertical number line is the
   - (A) y-axis.
   - (B) x-axis.
   - (C) angle.
   - (D) coordinate.

8. The first number in an ordered pair is the
   - (F) denominator.
   - (G) sum.
   - (H) x-coordinate.
   - (J) y-coordinate.

9. On a coordinate plane, the axes meet at the
   - (A) center.
   - (B) coordinate.
   - (C) origin.
   - (D) angle.

Solve for x.

10. $x - 19 = 41$
    - (F) 20
    - (G) 22
    - (H) 60
    - (J) 28

11. $4x + 15 = -5$
    - (A) –10
    - (B) –5
    - (C) 11
    - (D) 5

12. $41 = 6x - 13$
    - (F) 9
    - (G) 18
    - (H) 12
    - (J) 6

> **STOP** ◄

Directions: Find the surface area of each figure. When appropriate, use π as equivalent to 3.14.

1.

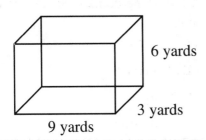

6 yards
3 yards
9 yards

- (A) 196 yds.²
- (B) 198 yds.²
- (C) 198 yds.
- (D) 427 yds.

4.

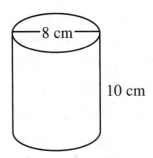

8 cm
10 cm

- (F) 351.68 cm²
- (G) 351.68 cm
- (H) 80 cm²
- (J) 800 cm

2.

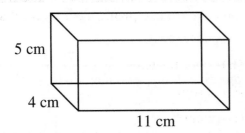

5 cm
4 cm
11 cm

- (F) 238 cm
- (G) 238 cm²
- (H) 210 cm
- (J) 210 cm²

5.

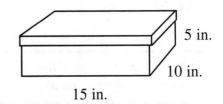

5 in.
10 in.
15 in.

- (A) 30 in.
- (B) 350 in.²
- (C) 550 in.²
- (D) 300 in.²

3.

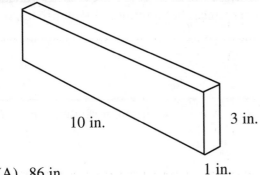

10 in.
3 in.
1 in.

- (A) 86 in.
- (B) 30 in.
- (C) 86 in.²
- (D) 40 in.²

6.

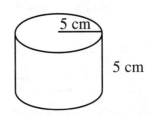

5 cm
5 cm

- (F) 25 cm²
- (G) 250 cm
- (H) 314 cm
- (J) 314 cm²

> STOP <

Mathematics: Statistics and Probability

Directions: Read each problem and choose the correct answer.

1. Lauren has a total of 17 dimes and nickels. The total value of the coins is $1.25. How many of each kind of coin does she have?

   (A) 6 dimes, 11 nickels

   (B) 10 dimes, 7 nickels

   (C) 7 dimes, 11 nickels

   (D) 8 dimes, 9 nickels

2. Ellen inspects games in a factory. She rejected 3 out of 80 because they were missing pieces. How many games would you think Ellen will reject in a shipment of 2,400?

   (F) about 90   (H) about 2,310

   (G) about 900   (J) about 2,000

3. Find the number of possible lunches when choosing 3 sandwiches, 2 potato chip bags, and 4 drinks.

   (A) 9   (C) 11

   (B) 20   (D) 24

4. Heidi has 3 quarters, 2 dimes, and 3 nickels in her pocket. She draws a coin at random. Find the probability of drawing a quarter or a nickel.

   (F) 5/56   (H) 1/4

   (G) 9/64   (J) 3/4

5. A drawer of socks contains 3 red, 4 blue, and 2 yellow. One sock is drawn at random. Find the *odds* in favor of drawing a red or a yellow sock.

   (A) 5 to 9   (C) 5 to 4

   (B) 5 to 24   (D) 1 to 4

6. The number cube is rolled 150 times. Find the number times that a number greater than 2 is expected to appear.

   (F) about 100   (H) about 25

   (G) about 125   (J) about 50

7. Each of the letters A, B, C, D, E, F is written on a card. A card is chosen at random. Find *P* (vowel).

   (A) 1/6   (C) 1/3

   (B) 1/2   (D) 2/3

8. Andrew rolls a number cube and tosses a penny. Find *P* (5, then heads).

   (F) 1/6   (H) 5/12

   (G) 1/12   (J) 5/36

≫ STOP ≪

Mean, Median, and Mode

Directions: Fill in the circle of the correct answer.

Find the MEAN of each set.

1. 0.8, 1.2, 0.75, 0.62, 0.88
   - (A) 0.75
   - (B) 0.85
   - (C) 0.6
   - (D) 0.87

2. 108, 97, 86, 99, 102, 90
   - (F) 97
   - (G) 86
   - (H) 88
   - (J) 183

3. 98.8, 99.5, 102.1, 101.5, 99.1
   - (A) 102.1
   - (B) 100
   - (C) 100.2
   - (D) 101

4. 4.50, 6.25, 5.25, 10, 8.75, 8.75
   - (F) 5.25
   - (G) 6.00
   - (H) 7.25
   - (J) 9.25

Find the MEDIAN of each set.

5. 142, 130, 223, 178, 129
   - (A) 142
   - (B) 220
   - (C) 185
   - (D) 178

6. 12.5, 13.4, 17.7, 20.2, 15.4, 16.1
   - (F) 17.7
   - (G) 15.75
   - (H) 19.5
   - (J) 20

7. 19, 17, 24, 23, 28, 35, 38
   - (A) 22
   - (B) 24
   - (C) 26
   - (D) 21.5

8. 72, 74, 68, 65, 70, 70, 68
   - (F) 65
   - (G) 68
   - (H) 70
   - (J) 69

Find the MODE OR MODES of each set.

9. 0.5, 0.33, 0.7, 0.61, 0.4
   - (A) no mode
   - (B) 0.7
   - (C) 0.33
   - (D) 10

10. 40, 35, 35, 38, 37, 42, 37
    - (F) 35 and 38
    - (G) 35 and 37
    - (H) 35
    - (J) 10 and 37

11. 3, 2, 4, 4, 3, 1, 2, 1, 5, 4, 6
    - (A) 4
    - (B) 3
    - (C) 3.5
    - (D) 5

12. 35, 54, 17, 18, 42, 44, 42, 61
    - (F) 42
    - (G) 18
    - (H) 17
    - (J) 18.5

 ➤ **STOP** ◄

Introduction

Science tries to uncover the physical truth about the way things work—how the seasons change, why animals hibernate, or what kinds of rock are created by volcanoes, for example. To perform your best on questions about science, you must pay attention to important words in each question that might make the answer choices true or untrue.

Here's the Idea

People who work in science try to find out what is true and what is untrue. Questions on science tests often have words in them, such as *not, but, except, always, never,* and *only,* which make answer choices true or untrue. You must watch for these key words in the test questions.

However, before we look at these key words, below are some tips that apply to taking any test, whether it is in language arts, mathematics, science, social studies, fine arts, or computers and technology. These tips will be repeated because they are important!

Test-Taking Tips

- **Read directions carefully before marking any test questions**, even though you have done that kind of test before. You may think you already know what the directions say, but don't ignore them—read them over. If you don't understand the directions, raise your hand and ask for help. Although your teacher must read the directions exactly as they are written, the teacher can make sure you understand what the directions mean.

- **Follow instructions.** Pay close attention to the sample exercises. They will help you understand what the items on the test will be like and how to mark your answer sheet properly.

- **Read the entire question and all the answer choices.** Do not stop reading when you have found a correct answer. Choices D or E may read "B and D" or "all of the above" or "none of the above." On some tests, two answers are both correct. You need to read all the answer choices before marking your answer.

- **For long reading passages, read the questions first so you know what to look for.** If you read the questions first, you'll find information in the passage that answers questions.

- **Remember that taking a test is not a race!** There are no prizes for finishing first. Use all of the time provided for the test. If you have time left over, check your answers.

Try and Discuss

Let's discuss those key words in many science questions: *not, but, except, always, never,* and *only.*
Words such as *not, but, except, always, never,* and *only* make a big difference, but you must be alert for
them. Look at these questions.

Which of the following is *not* part of the circulatory system?

(A) heart

(B) bones

(C) blood vessels

(D) blood

Fill in the correct circle.

Ⓐ   Ⓑ   Ⓒ   Ⓓ

At first glance, "blood" might seem like the odd one here because it is a liquid; it is not a solid object
like the others. But read the question carefully: "Which of the following is *not* part of the circulatory
system?" It's not asking "Which one does not belong?" The circulatory system does not include
bones, so (B) "bones" is the correct answer.

Now look at the following question:

Which of the following is *not* an example of fungi?

(A) mold

(B) mushrooms

(C) mildew

(D) dirt

Fill in the correct circle.

Ⓐ   Ⓑ   Ⓒ   Ⓓ

Mold, mildew, and dirt all seem like unpleasant things at first glance. So you might think, as you let
your eye go over the list, that "mushroom" is the odd one here—at least you can eat mushrooms. But
look closely at the question: "Which of the following is *not* an example of fungi?" Mushrooms,
mildew, and mold are all part of one group—they are all fungi. Dirt is the odd one—it is not a fungus.
A lot depends on that part of the question, "*not* an example of fungi."

Tips That Help

Remember the following:

- People who work in science try to find out what is true and untrue.

- Pay attention to key words in science questions, such as *not, but, except, always, never,* and *only,*
  that will make answer choices true or untrue.

 Now try the practice tests, listening to your teacher's directions.

Directions: Fill in the circle beside the term or terms that DO NOT belong.

Sample
Cell processes

(A) osmosis   (B) photosynthesis   (C) reptiles   (D) mitosis

1. Five kingdom classification

   (A) monera   (B) measurement   (C) viruses   (D) bacteria

2. Disease

   (F) immunity   (G) vaccinations   (H) natural defenses   (J) respiration

3. Cold blooded vertebrates

   (A) dogs   (B) fish   (C) reptiles   (D) amphibians

4. Human nutrition and digestion

   (F) nutrients   (G) four food groups   (H) molds   (J) diet

5. Heart and circulation

   (A) skeletal system   (B) capillaries   (C) pulmonary   (D) coronary

6. Respiration and excretion

   (F) skin   (G) perspiration   (H) waste   (J) muscular system

7. Algae

   (A) mosses   (B) oaks   (C) liverworts   (D) ferns

8. Nonseed plants

   (F) vascular   (G) gymnosperms   (H) corn   (J) angiosperm

9. The environment

   (A) biotic   (B) biosphere   (C) ecosystem   (D) transportation

GO →

10. Properties of matter

    (F) elements   (G) support   (H) mixtures   (J) compounds

11. The atom

    (A) periodic table   (B) photosynthesis   (C) mass   (D) number

12. Chemical compounds

    (F) wood   (G) ionic   (H) covalent   (J) formula

13. Mixtures

    (A) suspensions   (B) colloids   (C) unsaturated   (D) diet

14. Gravity and motion

    (F) momentum   (G) velocity   (H) atomic   (J) mass

15. Waves and sound

    (A) reflection   (B) subtraction   (C) diffraction   (D) defraction

16. The Earth-Moon system

    (F) tides   (G) phases   (H) poetry   (J) movements

17. Planets of the solar system

    (A) meteorites   (B) comets   (C) orbit   (D) rockets

18. Geologic time

    (F) fossils   (G) era   (H) sun   (J) sedimentary

19. Geology

    (A) oceans   (B) mantle   (C) core   (D) magma

20. Weather

    (F) beach   (G) fronts   (H) air masses   (J) pressure

➤ **STOP** ◄

Directions: Choose the correct answer for each question.

1. Which is the BEST definition of "atmosphere"?

   (A) It is air.

   (B) It is invisible pressure caused by gravity.

   (C) It is the mass of gases that surrounds a planet or other heavenly body.

   (D) It is the blue in the sky.

2. Which is NOT one of the layers of Earth's atmosphere?

   (F) the troposphere   (H) the stratosphere

   (G) the biosphere   (J) the thermosphere

3. Which is NOT correct?

   (A) The earth's gravity holds the air in place around the earth.

   (B) Air carries tiny water droplets.

   (C) Clouds are made of hot steam.

   (D) Sunlight makes the sky blue.

4. Which is NOT one of the gases in Earth's atmosphere?

   (F) nitrogen   (H) carbon monoxide

   (G) oxygen   (J) ozone

5. Which is NOT correct?

   (A) When we breathe, we take in oxygen from the air and give off carbon dioxide.

   (B) We are using up oxygen as a natural resource.

   (C) Green plants take in carbon dioxide and give off oxygen.

   (D) Most fuels must have oxygen to burn.

6. Which is the ONLY correct statement?

   (F) The greenhouse effect is always harmful.

   (G) Ozone is poisonous.

   (H) Ozone absorbs many of the sun's harmful ultraviolet rays.

   (J) Water vapor is not needed to produce rain and snow.

7. The amount of moisture in the air is known as

   (A) pressure.   (C) fog.

   (B) temperature.   (D) humidity.

8. Which is NOT correct?

   (F) Warm air holds more moisture than cool air.

   (G) Water vapor enters the air when water evaporates from bodies of water.

   (H) Moisture in the air is in the form of water vapor.

   (J) There is less moisture in the air on cloudy days.

GO →

9. When water vapor begins to change to tiny water droplets or ice crystals, this process is called

(A) moisturizing.   (C) evaporation.

(B) humidifying.   (D) condensation.

10. Beads of water form on blades of grass because the air near the surface of the ground has cooled below the

(F) freezing point.   (H) moisturizing point.

(G) dew point.   (J) leveling-off point.

11. Which is the ONLY correct statement?

(A) When the relative humidity reaches 100 percent, the air is completely dry.

(B) When the relative humidity reaches 100 percent, the air is holding as much moisture as possible.

(C) Humidity is the same everywhere in the United States.

(D) There has to be no humidity for it to snow.

12. As air rises, its temperature

(F) increases.   (H) stays the same.

(G) decreases.   (J) air doesn't rise.

13. Which of the following is NOT a true statement?

(A) Clouds form when large masses of moist air rise and are cooled below the dew point.

(B) Every cloud consists of air filled with water droplets or ice crystals.

(C) Fog is simply a cloud near the earth's surface.

(D) Rain cannot change into snow.

14. Which is NOT a true statement?

(F) Particles enter the air from active volcanoes, automobile exhaust, and fires.

(G) The wind carries particles of dust and sand up from the ground into the atmosphere.

(H) Particles remain floating in the air forever.

(J) Rain and snow washes particles out of the air.

15. An instrument used to measure air pressure is a

(A) thermometer.   (C) barometer.

(B) millibar.   (D) weather vane.

16. What would happen in the following experiment? You remove air from a bottle and seal it. You weigh the bottle. You break the seal and let air rush in. You weigh the bottle again.

(F) The bottle will weigh less.

(G) The bottle will weigh the same because air is weightless.

(H) The bottle will weigh more.

(J) The weight of the bottle will change as air swirls around in it.

GO →

17. Which is NOT true of air pollution?

    (A) Air pollution occurs when wastes dirty the air.

    (B) Pollution can cause health problems.

    (C) Pollution has no effect on nonliving things such as buildings and water.

    (D) Pollution damages the earth's atmosphere.

18. All of the following are air pollutants EXCEPT

    (F) carbon monoxide.   (H) hydrocarbons.

    (G) nitrogen.   (J) nitrogen oxides.

19. Which is NOT a correct statement?

    (A) Ozone in the upper atmosphere makes life possible on Earth.

    (B) Chlorofluorocarbons destroy the ozone layer.

    (C) Overexposure to ultraviolet rays is a cause of skin cancer.

    (D) Smog would occur naturally without people.

True or False

20. There is less air on a mountaintop than at sea level.

    (A) True   (B) False

21. Your ears "pop" in an elevator going up a tall building or in an airplane because of an increase of air pressure.

    (A) True   (B) False

22. Wind is caused by clouds blowing.

    (A) True   (B) False

23. Fast-moving winds high above Earth are called jet streams.

    (A) True   (B) False

24. Air resistance is what makes a parachute jumper fall slowly to Earth.

    (A) True   (B) False

25. Air resistance decreases the faster you go on your bike.

    (A) True   (B) False

26. Meteoroids burn up in above the earth because they are not made to exist in our atmosphere.

    (A) True   (B) False

27. Most air pollution comes from human activities.

    (A) True   (B) False

28. Because of increased gases in the air, the greenhouse effect is causing temperatures on earth to rise.

    (A) True   (B) False   ➤ **STOP** ◄

Directions: Fill in the circle next to the term that would complete the sentence correctly.

_____ are naturally occurring inorganic solids that are formed in the earth. They all have definite
   1

chemical compositions: they are either elements or _____. Most on the earth's surface are
                                                    2

_____. These contain silicon and oxygen, the two most abundant elements on Earth's crust.
   3

      (A) silicates   (B) minerals   (C) carbonates   (D) compounds

Rocks begin as mixtures of minerals that form from the cooling of the Earth's _____. Upon
                                                                4

cooling, this substance forms _____ rock. _____ rocks can include organic material.
                                         5   6

This type of rock is often formed by rivers and oceans.

      (F) sedimentary   (G) magma   (H) igneous   (J) granite

The solid earth is called the geosphere. The outer layer, where we live, is called the _____.
                                                           7

Beneath the surface on which we stand are two other layers, first the _____ and deeper is the _____.
                                                 8   9

      (A) spheroid   (B) crust   (C) core   (D) mantle

The continents and oceans are floating on pieces of the earth's lithosphere. Pieces of the lithosphere

are called _____. When these shift, they often cause _____ or volcanoes. The magma
            10   11

that flows out of volcanoes is called _____.
                                      12

      (F) lava   (G) plates   (H) earthquakes   (J) vibrations

Fossils are evidences of _____. A fossil can be a complete _____ imprinted in limestone, or just
                              13   14

a leaf or footprint. Most fossils are found in _____ rock.
                                           15

      (A) sedimentary   (B) past life   (C) prehistoric   (D) organism

➤ STOP ◄

Directions: Choose the correct answer for each question.

1. Which is NOT correct?
   (A) The cell is the basic unit of all life.
   (B) All living things are made up of cells.
   (C) Some organisms consist of only one cell.
   (D) All cells are either male or female.

2. All cells have the following in common EXCEPT
   (F) a cell is alive.
   (G) if left unharmed, it will live forever.
   (H) it "breathes," takes in food, and gets rid of wastes.
   (J) it also grows and reproduces.

Identify the parts of a cell.

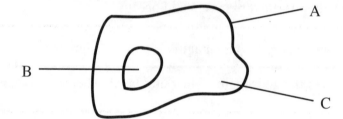

   3. membrane
   4. nucleus
   5. cytoplasm

6. Which is NOT a kind of cell?
   (F) amoeba
   (G) diatoms
   (H) pyramids
   (J) bacteria

7. Which is NOT correct?
   (A) DNA makes up the genes, the basic units of heredity.
   (B) Genes control the passing on of characteristics from parents to offspring.
   (C) In some cases, one animal can give birth to a completely different kind of animal.
   (D) The chemical structure of DNA determines your blood type, the color of your eyes, and the texture of your hair, for example.

8. All cells can be seen with the naked eye.
   (A) True   (B) False

9. Every new cell is produced from another cell.
   (A) True   (B) False

GO →

10. All the cells in your body are the same kind of cell.

    (A) True   (B) False

11. When a cell divides, each of the two newly produced cells gets a copy of the genetic program.

    (A) True   (B) False

12. Blood is red because there are only red blood cells.

    (A) True   (B) False

13. The genetic program is contained in a chemical substance called DNA.

    (A) True   (B) False

14. Chromosomes are in the nucleus of a cell.

    (A) True   (B) False

15. Human beings and other multicellular organisms also develop from a single cell.

    (A) True   (B) False

16. Asexual reproduction involves two parents.

    (A) True   (B) False

17. In human beings, chromosomes known as X and Y chromosomes determine an individual's sex.

    (A) True   (B) False

18. A dominant gene will hide the effects of a recessive gene.

    (A) True   (B) False

➤ **STOP** ◄

Science: Properties of Matter

Directions: Choose the correct answer for each question.

1. Which is NOT true of matter?
   (A) It is the substance of which all things are made.
   (B) It is anything that occupies space.
   (C) It is always solid.
   (D) It has mass.

2. When matter goes out into space, away from Earth, it loses its weight. Therefore, _____ gives matter its weight.
   (F) solidity
   (G) atmosphere
   (H) gravity
   (J) the solar system

3. When wood burns, matter changes into
   (A) a gas.
   (B) energy.
   (C) particles.
   (D) none of the above.

4. Which is NOT an example of the physical properties of matter?
   (F) color
   (G) odor
   (H) mass
   (J) ability to rust

5. Substances that can be broken down by chemical change into simpler elements are called
   (A) mixtures.   (C) compounds.
   (B) chemicals.   (D) crystals.

6. Which is NOT part of an atom?
   (F) protons   (H) electrons
   (G) neutrinos   (J) neutrons

7. Atoms form larger particles called
   (A) molecules.
   (B) bonds.
   (C) building blocks.
   (D) models.

GO →

8. Most of the compounds found in living organisms contain the element
   (F) water.
   (G) carbon.
   (H) plasma.
   (J) chlorophyll.

9. Molecules are bound together by
   (A) hydrogen.
   (B) orbits.
   (C) electrical force.
   (D) rings.

10. Which is NOT a physical state of matter?
    (F) electric
    (G) solid
    (H) liquid
    (J) gas

Matching

11. atoms arranged in regular patterns
12. does not change shape easily
13. exerts pressure equally in all directions
14. has form
15. has low densities
16. has the ability to flow
17. has no shape of its own
18. takes the shape of any container in which it is placed

(A) a solid
(B) a liquid
(C) a gas

True or False

19. Each chemical element is made up of only one kind of atom.
    (A) True   (B) False

20. Chemists use letters of the alphabet as symbols for the elements.
    (A) True   (B) False

21. When atoms collide, molecules are created.
    (A) True   (B) False

22. Compound is a substance that contains more than one kind of atom.
    (A) True   (B) False

➤ **STOP** ◄

Directions: Read the passage below, and choose the correct answer to each question. (*Testing tip:* read the questions first so you know what to look for.)

Plants and animals conduct activities at specific times during a single rotation of the earth around the sun or every 24 hours. For example, ground squirrels are active during the day, but flying squirrels are active during the night. Male crickets chirp at the same time each evening. These organisms might seem to be responding only to light or darkness. But scientists say that is not true.

Light in the morning and darkness in the evening are cyclic; in other words, they repeat each 24 hours—an *environmental clock*. In the same way, scientists also conclude that plants and animals have an internal mechanism within the systems of their bodies called a *biological clock*. By chemical means, the biological clock causes behavior and physiological activities at certain times during a 24-hour period, and these activities repeat themselves each 24 hours—like a clock. These activities are called *rhythms*. For example, the biological clock regulates the rhythms of flowers opening, the times of hamster activities, the mating of certain species of fruit flies, and the times that crickets chirp.

It is critical that rhythms of the biological clock match rhythms of the environmental clock. If they didn't, day-pollinated flowers would open at night and insects that pollinate these plants would be asleep. But the existence of two clocks—environmental and biological—also raise several questions. First, are the two clocks exactly matched—in other words, do certain insects always sleep in darkness, or do the two clocks work independently of one another? But if the two clocks work independently of one another, how do they get "in sync"? That's to say, how do biological creatures match their rhythms to the environmental clock?

Crickets were insects chosen to test these questions. The male crickets usually begin to chirp at sunset. The first test had to do with clock independence. Does darkness (an event on the environmental clock) cause crickets to chirp (an event on the biological clock)? Crickets were removed from their ordinary cycle of 12-hours light and 12-hours darkness and placed into a chamber with 24 hours of continuous light. The result? Chirping continued at the same time throughout 24-hour periods of continuous light. This result proved the independence of the two clocks, meaning that darkness does not automatically start the chirping in crickets.

But something unexpected happened, too. While the "no darkness" experiments were being run, the beginning of chirping started later and later during each 24-hour period. In other words, the time of chirping began to drift. This showed that the environmental and biological clocks were gradually matching less and less. However, when the crickets were removed from continuous light and put back in a normal cycle of 12-hours of light/12-hours of dark, the start of the chirping shifted back to its original pattern: the crickets began chirping when it got dark again. Chirping, which was regulated by the biological clock, once again matched the start of darkness, which is an event on the environmental clock. That match is important because the female cricket makes an appearance at the onset of darkness. It is clear then that the chirps of the male cricket at night are meant to attract the female for mating purposes.

GO →

Scientists realized that the change from light to dark on the environmental clock is the cue setting the biological clock. The cricket sees the change in light. A nerve signal travels to the cricket's brain where the event—the change from light to dark—and the event, chirping, are matched, and the result is that the two clocks run together. The cricket would chirp about every 24 hours anyway, but without the beginning of darkness, the cricket's start time begins to be off.

There is good reason for the biological clock. Environmental events happen regularly day after day, night after night. The biological clock prepares the body to get ready and respond to these events. In other words, the body's chemistry is set and ready for action every 24 hours.

1. It is important to survival that rhythms match in the world.
   (A) True
   (B) False

2. The two clocks, environmental and biological, will match no matter what happens.
   (A) True
   (B) False

3. The purpose of the cricket experiment was to find out if
   (A) crickets will not chirp unless it gets dark.
   (B) crickets will sleep in daylight.
   (C) the two clocks run together or separately.
   (D) there are reasons for crickets to chirp.

4. The reason crickets chirp at night is
   (F) to attract female crickets.
   (G) to announce that day is over.
   (H) to set their biological clocks.
   (J) to control their environment.

5. The crickets started chirping every 24 hours even with no darkness because
   (A) of the environmental clock.
   (B) because of the biological clock.
   (C) because they were caged.
   (D) because scientists were testing them.

6. What gets the environmental clock and the biological clock running together is
   (F) instinct.
   (G) food.
   (H) darkness.
   (J) light.

7. A good title for this passage would be
   (A) Crickets are Unpredictable.
   (B) The Two Clocks of Nature.
   (C) Light or Dark: It Doesn't Make Any Difference.
   (D) What the Cricket Sees.

➤ STOP ◄

Introduction

Social studies is all about people and places. It can be difficult at times to remember many names and events. But to perform your best on a social studies section, it helps to ask yourself a question about the question!

Here's the Idea

A social studies question may be about a region, a president, or an event. It helps focus your attention on what the question is asking—and it helps you eliminate choices, too—if you ask yourself *who, what, where, when*, or *how*.

However, before we look at these key words, below are some tips that apply to taking any test, whether it is in language arts, mathematics, science, social studies, fine arts, or computers and technology. These tips are repeated because they are important!

Test-Taking Tips

- **Read directions carefully before marking any test questions**, even though you have done that kind of test before. You may think you already know what the directions say, but don't ignore them—read them over. If you don't understand the directions, raise your hand and ask for help. Although your teacher must read the directions exactly as they are written, the teacher can make sure you understand what the directions mean.

- **Follow instructions.** Pay close attention to the sample exercises. They will help you understand what the items on the test will be like and how to mark your answer sheet properly.

- **Read the entire question and all the answer choices.** Do not stop reading when you have found a correct answer. Choices D or E may read "B and D" or "all of the above" or "none of the above." On some tests, two answers are both correct. You need to read all the answer choices before marking your answer.

- **For long reading passages, read the questions first so you know what to look for.** If you read the questions first, you'll find information in the passage that answers questions.

- **Remember that taking a test is not a race!** There are no prizes for finishing first. Use all of the time provided for the test. If you have time left over, check your answers.

Try and Discuss

Let's discuss asking the questions *who, what, where, when,* or *how.* Social studies questions are about persons, places, or events and when or how they happened.

For example, here's a social studies test question:

A major industry of the Midwest region is

Fill in the correct circle.

(A) agriculture.
(B) Illinois, Ohio, Wisconsin, Iowa, and Michigan.
(C) fishing.
(D) the Civil War.

Ⓐ   Ⓑ   Ⓒ   Ⓓ

Ask yourself, "Is this a question about *who, what, where, when,* or *how*?" It asks about "a major industry." It is asking *what,* <u>not</u> *where,* which eliminates choice (B) right away. The correct answer is (A) "agriculture."

Look at the list of topics below. Would they probably be asking *who, what, where, when,* or *how*? (You may be right sometimes if you suggest more than one.)

- maps

- climate

- resources

- people

- history

Tips That Help

Social studies is all about people and places. It can be difficult at times to remember lots of names and events. But to perform your best on a social studies section, it helps to ask yourself a question about the question: *who, what, where, when,* or *how.*

 Now try the practice tests, listening to your teacher's directions.

Ancient Egypt

Directions: In this section, there are key words about Ancient Egypt. Read the definition and choose the correct term.

1. Stretch of dangerous rapids in the Nile.
   - (A) falls
   - (B) cataracts
   - (C) pools
   - (D) current

2. A god or goddess. Many Egyptian ones can have human, semi-human, and animal shapes.
   - (F) deity
   - (G) statue
   - (H) sun
   - (J) Nile

3. A series of rulers, usually related to each other by blood or marriage.
   - (A) supreme
   - (B) dynasty
   - (C) thrones
   - (D) generations

4. The oldest Egyptian script: most are pictures of people, animals, plants or things. The word is Greek and means "sacred carving."
   - (F) cuneiform
   - (G) runes
   - (H) hieroglyphic
   - (J) signs

5. The artificial preservation of bodies. Drying out the body was usually the most important process.
   - (A) entombment
   - (B) embalming
   - (C) mummification
   - (D) sacred rites

6. A Greek term meaning "City of the Dead." It is used for large and important burials. These were mainly on the edge of the desert.
   - (F) necropolis
   - (G) acropolis
   - (H) valley
   - (J) underworld

7. A tapering stone shaft with a tip shaped like a pyramid. A symbol of the sun's rays. Pairs were often set up outside temples.
   - (A) columns
   - (B) obelisk
   - (C) banners
   - (D) gates

8. A shrine where a god or goddess answered questions from worshippers.
   - (F) throne
   - (G) pyramid
   - (H) oracle
   - (J) Valley of the Kings

9. A marsh plant and a type of paper made from it. Also a scroll made from sheets of this paper gummed together.
   - (A) reed
   - (B) cattail
   - (C) wheat
   - (D) papyrus

10. A title for the king of Egypt from the late 18th dynasty onwards. It means "The Great House."
    - (F) deity
    - (G) pharaoh
    - (H) Zoraster
    - (J) Highness

11. A stone chest that a coffin was placed in: rectangular or human body-shaped.
    - (A) sarcophagus
    - (B) tomb
    - (C) pyramid
    - (D) grave

12. A person trained to read and write. Most worked for the government like secretaries or clerks.
    - (F) rabbi
    - (G) scribe
    - (H) scarab
    - (J) soldier

➤ **STOP** ◄

Ancient Greece

Directions: Match the term on the right with the definition on the left.

1. city-state	(A) what the Greeks called themselves		
2. best-known city-states	(B) the southern part of the mainland of Greece		
3. Hellenes	(C) the Golden Age		
4. barbarians	(D) consisted of a city or town and the surrounding villages and farmland		
5. Greece in the mid-400s B.C.	(F) non-Greeks		
6. seas on either side of the Greek peninsula	(G) fortified hill for defense		
7. the Peloponnesus	(H) Athens and Sparta		
8. acropolis	(J) the Aegean and the Ionian		

9. agora	(A) an open area that served as a market place and meeting place
10. colonies	(B) natural resources in Greece
11. limestone and marble	(C) gods and goddesses
12. a tough, warlike people	(D) where the gods and goddesses live
13. deities	(F) shrines where priests and priestesses foretold the future
14. oracles	(G) what the Greeks established around the Mediterranean
15. Mount Olympus	(H) Spartans
16. Zeus and Hera	(J) rulers over the other gods

17. held every four years in honor of Zeus	(A) oligarchy
18. philosophy	(B) Olympic Games
19. Socrates	(C) first major civilization near Greece
20. Doric, Ionian, and Corinthian	(D) sentenced to death for showing disrespect to the gods
21. rule by a few powerful, usually wealthy people	(F) a battle formation used by the Greeks that resembles a square
22. phalanx	(G) three most popular styles of Greek columns
23. Crete	(H) scene of the legendary battle written about by the poet Homer
24. Troy	(J) means "love of wisdom"

25. tyrant	(A) trial by jury, drama, democracy, philosophy, science
26. Delian League	(B) the 400s B.C. when Greek culture was at its highest
27. the Golden Age	(C) Greek term for leader who seizes power by force
28. the Peloponnesian War	(D) period between Alexander's death and conquest by the Romans
29. the Hellenistic Age	(F) ruinous conflict between Sparta and Athens
30. Alexander the Great	(G) created a Greek empire from Greece to India
31. Greek influences on Western civilization	(H) the power in the Mediterranean that came after Greece
32. Rome	(J) an alliance of the city-states during the 400s B.C.

➤ **STOP** ◄

Ancient Rome

Directions: Match the column on the left with the column on the right.

1. the Italian Peninsula
2. Latin
3. roads, bridges, and aqueducts
4. on seven wooded hills along the Tiber River
5. citizens and slaves
6. paterfamilias
7. Ceres, Janus, Jupiter
8. tunics and togas

(A) examples of Roman gods
(B) where the Roman Empire began
(C) Roman building achievements
(D) the two main social classes of Rome
(F) Roman clothes
(G) father of the family
(H) the language of the Ancient Romans
(J) where the city of Rome was located

---

9. atrium
10. Coliseum
11. gladiators
12. charioteers
13. circus
14. pantomimes
15. gymnasiums
16. Acta Diura

(A) a courtyard in the center of a wealthy Roman's home
(B) trained warriors who performed
(C) exercise rooms
(D) long oval arena
(F) stories told through music and dancing
(G) the government newspaper posted daily in Rome
(H) skilled horsemen who raced for entertainment
(J) enormous amphitheater in Rome

---

17. portico
18. the arch and concrete
19. vaults
20. Ptolemy
21. Galen
22. two consuls
23. Senate
24. patricians

(A) a Greek physician who insisted medicine come from experiments
(B) arched roofs
(C) covered walkway
(D) the most powerful government body of the Republic
(F) members of Rome's oldest and richest families
(G) leaders of the government in the days of the Republic
(H) two engineering feats that made big Roman structures possible
(J) inventor of a system of astronomy in use for 1,500 years

---

25. plebeians
26. tribunes
27. emperors
28. Carthage
29. alliances and pride in organization
30. Caesar
31. Christianity
32. Vandals and Visigoths

(A) two main reasons for Roman success
(B) supreme leaders with total authority during the Roman
(C) important reason for civil disorder in the late empire
(D) ordinary Roman citizens
(F) leaders of the citizens' assembly
(G) Germanic tribes who conquered Rome
(H) ended the Republic by becoming sole ruler of the Roman world
(J) Rome's early rival for power and trade in the Mediterranean

➤ **STOP** ◄

Social Studies: World Geography

Directions: Choose the correct answer for each question.

1. Halfway between the poles of Earth is an imaginary circle called the
   (A) globe.
   (B) equator.
   (C) international date line.
   (D) Van Allen Belt.

2. The approximate circumference of Earth is
   (F) 25,000 miles.   (H) 100,000 miles.
   (G) 10,000 miles.   (J) 1,000 miles.

3. Earth is not round. The best way to describe it is
   (A) apple-shaped.
   (B) basketball-shaped.
   (C) oblong.
   (D) pear-shaped.

4. The air above and surrounding Earth is called the
   (F) ozone layer.   (H) sky.
   (G) atmosphere.   (J) biosphere.

5. Earth's surface is about 70 percent
   (A) land.   (C) water.
   (B) nitrogen.   (D) populated.

6. The highest land on the planet is
   (F) Mount McKinley.
   (G) Mount Rushmore.
   (H) Mount Everest.
   (J) Pike's Peak.

7. The largest bodies of land are called
   (A) shelves.
   (B) mountains.
   (C) plates.
   (D) continents.

8. The world's largest ocean is the
   (F) Indian.   (H) Atlantic.
   (G) Pacific.   (J) Arctic.

9. The world's largest area of fresh water is
   (A) the Great Lakes in the United States.
   (B) the Caspian Sea.
   (C) the Black Sea.
   (D) Lake Tahoe.

10. The world's longest river is the
    (F) Nile.   (H) Amazon.
    (G) Mississippi.   (J) Missouri.

11. Most of the world's population lives on
    (A) plateaus.
    (B) mountains.
    (C) hills and plains.
    (D) tundra.

12. Map making or studying maps is called
    (F) geology.
    (G) geography.
    (H) archeology.
    (J) cartography.

13. Which is NOT a term associated with flat maps?
    (A) projection   (C) Mercator
    (B) distortion   (D) globe

14. The kinds of maps that show the earth's features are called _____ maps.
    (F) topographic
    (G) general reference
    (H) navigation
    (J) political

GO →

15. _____ list and explain the symbols and colors used on a map.

   (A) Map legends

   (B) Indexes

   (C) Coordinates

   (D) Glossaries

16. _____ shows how the distances on a map reduce the real distances on Earth.

   (F) Direction

   (G) Compass

   (H) Survey

   (J) Scale

17. Parallels are imaginary circles around the globe that measure

   (A) distance.

   (B) latitude.

   (C) hours.

   (D) time.

18. _____ extend from the North Pole to the South Pole, forming half-circles indicating longitude.

   (F) Degrees

   (G) Compass points

   (H) Charts

   (J) Meridians

Directions: Match the terms on the left with the definitions on the right.

19. glacier   (A) the shallow part of the seabed bordering most continents

20. plateau   (B) a lowland between hills or mountains usually with a river or stream

21. delta   (C) the deposit of earth that collect at the mouths of some rivers

22. tundra   (D) a large mass of ice that moves slowly down a mountain or slope

23. continental shelf   (F) a vast, level treeless plain in the arctic regions

24. desert   (G) a barren region with little or no rainfall, usually sandy

25. valley   (H) a narrow valley with high steep sides

26. canyon   (J) a plain in the mountains

➤ **STOP** ◄

Early Exploration

Directions: Choose the correct answer for each question.

True or False

1. Most likely, the first people wandered into North America across a land bridge from Asia.
   (A) True   (B) False

2. The Vikings were probably the first European people to reach America.
   (A) True   (B) False

3. The Spanish introduced civilization to the Aztecs, Incas, and Mayans.
   (A) True   (B) False

4. During the 1600s, Europeans became interested in finding a short sea route to the Far East.
   (A) True   (B) False

5. Which is NOT correct?
   (A) The Spanish and Portuguese controlled the land from Mexico south.
   (B) The French established settlements in Canada.
   (C) The Germans claimed the Dakotas.
   (D) The English established settlements in New England.

6. The first permanent English settlement was at
   (F) New Amsterdam.
   (G) Jamestown, Virginia.
   (H) The Outer Banks of Carolina.
   (J) Providence, Rhode Island.

Directions: Match the explorers with their exploits.

7. Columbus   (A) French explorer who founded Quebec

8. John Cabot   (B) credited with discovering a New World

9. Amerigo Vespucci   (C) Italian for whom a continent was named

10. Balboa   (D) claimed the Mississippi Valley for France

11. Champlain   (F) saw the Pacific Ocean from Panama

12. Joliett and Marquette   (G) conqueror of the Aztecs

13. La Salle   (H) explored the coast of Maine and eastern Canada

14. Cortez   (J) canoed up to end of the Mississippi   ➤ **STOP** ◄

Pre-Revolutionary America

Directions: Choose the correct answer to each question.

1. The first English colony in America disappeared. It was at
   - (A) Jamestown, Virginia.
   - (B) Hudson Bay.
   - (C) Chesapeake Bay.
   - (D) Roanoke, North Carolina.

2. Which was NOT true of the early colonists?
   - (F) They were not very well prepared.
   - (G) They broke away from England immediately.
   - (H) They prospered slowly.
   - (J) They valued hard work, religion, and freedom.

3. In the early 1600s, the English king began granting _____ for the purpose of establishing colonies in America.
   - (A) armies
   - (B) charters
   - (C) joint-stock companies
   - (D) tickets

4. Which is NOT a true statement?
   - (F) Colonists at Jamestown were sent there to find gold and valuable items.
   - (G) Maryland was started as a place for Catholics.
   - (H) Pennsylvania was founded by a Quaker.
   - (J) Florida was the last of the thirteen colonies.

5. The Puritans settled in Massachusetts Bay because
   - (A) they planned to convert the Indians to Christianity.
   - (B) they wanted to practice their faith separately.
   - (C) they had been expelled from England.
   - (D) they signed on to ships as indentured servants.

6. Who was NOT a Puritan leader?
   - (F) William Bradford
   - (G) John Winthrop
   - (H) William Penn
   - (J) Roger Williams

7. An early document created by the Puritans that captured their desire for democracy and equality was the
   - (A) Port Huron Statement.
   - (B) Articles of Confederation.
   - (C) Mayflower Compact.
   - (D) Friendship Accords.

GO →

Pre-Revolutionary America *(cont.)*

8. Under the guidance of William Penn, _____ became the largest city in colonial America and later the nation's capital.

   (F) Trenton   (H) New York

   (G) Philadelphia   (J) Charleston

9. Which of the following was NOT a crop that encouraged the use of slaves?

   (A) rice   (C) tobacco

   (B) indigo   (D) corn

10. Which was NOT a reason people came to the American colonies?

    (F) religious freedom

    (G) to become United States citizens

    (H) to get rich

    (J) because they had no choice: they were slaves or prisoners

11. If free people couldn't pay their transportation to the colonies, one option was to come as a(n)

    (A) loyalist.

    (B) indentured servant.

    (C) soldier.

    (D) doctor.

12. Slavery became more common in the South than the North because of

    (F) the heat.

    (G) seaports.

    (H) plantations.

    (J) law-breaking.

13. Which is a CORRECT description of the relationship between the American colonies and Britain?

    (A) Britain sent the colonists everything they needed to prosper.

    (B) The colonists worked for awhile in America and then returned to Britain.

    (C) The colonies sent Britain raw materials such as lumber, rice, or iron, and received finished products such as cookware or rifles in return.

    (D) Britain set up factories in the colonies and paid people to work in them.

14. Which is NOT true about society in the American colonies.

    (F) There were rich and poor people.

    (G) Land was easy and plentiful to obtain.

    (H) Hard work usually resulted in success.

    (J) Most people were illiterate and uneducated.

15. Which was the American colonial attitude about government?

    (A) Acting like a British subject was very important.

    (B) Government belonged to the people.

    (C) The best leaders were descendents of royalty.

    (D) Government was unnecessary and foolish.

➤ **STOP** ◄

The American Revolution

Directions: Match the dates on the time line with the correct events.

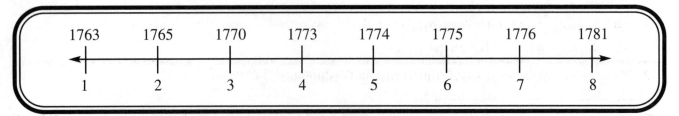

    1763   1765   1770   1773   1774   1775   1776   1781

     1   2   3   4   5   6   7   8

(A) Colonists adopt the Declaration of Independence and form the United States of America.

(B) Britain defeats France in the French and Indian War.

(C) The First Continental Congress meets to consider action against the British.

(D) British troops kill American civilians in the Boston Massacre.

(F) Colonists stage the Boston Tea Party, throwing British tea into Boston Harbor.

(G) The Revolutionary War begins.

(H) American army defeats the British at Yorktown, Virginia, the last major battle of the Revolutionary War.

(J) The British Parliament passes the Stamp Act, taxing printed matter in the colonies.

Directions: Match the event on the left with what happened as a result on the right.

9. British win the French and Indian War.

10. Quartering Act, Sugar Act, Stamp Act are passed.

11. Britain sends troops into New York City and Boston.

12. Colonists stage the Boston Tea Party and destroy tea.

13. First Continental Congress meets insisting repeal of Intolerable Acts.

14. British troops try to seize colonial arms in Massachusetts.

15. Thomas Paine publishes "Common Sense," a call for independence.

16. Americans win a decisive victory at Yorktown.

(A) Britain gained control of Canada, and all French territory east of the Mississippi River except New Orleans.

(B) Many colonists read the argument and are convinced.

(C) King George says colonies must obey or be crushed.

(D) Colonists mock the troops in Boston and provoke a riot.

(F) Colonists halt the British at Lexington and Concord, Massachusetts.

(G) Colonists bitterly oppose British policies.

(H) Britain passes the Intolerable Acts, closing Boston Harbor.

(J) The Treaty of Paris is signed in 1783.

➤ **STOP** ◄

The Constitution

Directions: Read the questions and choose the correct answer.

1. The Articles of Confederation were considered too weak to govern the United States.

   (A) True   (B) False

2. The framers of the new Constitution met in Washington, D.C.

   (A) True   (B) False

3. The Constitution provides for a three-house legislature: the House, the Senate, and the Supreme Court.

   (A) True   (B) False

4. The Constitution provides for three branches of government: the legislative, the executive, and the judiciary or court system.

   (A) True   (B) False

5. The point of the Bill of Rights was to guarantee individual rights.

   (A) True   (B) False

6. Rights stated in the Bill of Rights include the right to declare war, the right to make treaties, and the right to levy taxes.

   (A) True   (B) False

7. "Implied powers" are ones not stated in the Constitution but suggested, such as the power for the federal government to print money.

   (A) True   (B) False

8. In fact, all powers are given to the federal government; the Constitution provides no powers for the states.

   (A) True   (B) False

9. In case of conflict, such as a state not allowing children to attend school, the national government has supreme power.

   (A) True   (B) False

10. The Supreme Court may rule that a law is unconstitutional, but the president has the final say whether it is or not.

    (A) True   (B) False

11. The Constitution may not be amended: it's permanent the way it is.

    (A) True   (B) False

12. Both Congress and the states have to ratify proposed amendments to the Constitution.

    (A) True   (B) False

➤ **STOP** ◄

Slavery and the Election of 1860

Directions: Read the question and choose the correct answer.

1. The first blacks in the American Colonies were brought in, like many lower-class whites, as
   (A) prisoners.
   (B) indentured servants.
   (C) farmers.
   (D) Puritans.

2. The first black African slaves in the American Colonies also arrived during the early
   (F) 1400s   (H) 1600s
   (G) 1800s   (J) 1900s

3. Typical plantation crops were rice, tobacco, sugar cane, and later
   (A) fruits.   (C) beans.
   (B) poultry.   (D) cotton.

4. Slaves in the North tended to work in
   (F) factories, homes, and shipyards.
   (G) newspapers and fruit stands.
   (H) plantations.
   (J) schools.

5. During the mid-1600s, the colonies began to pass laws called slave codes. All of the following were prohibited by the slave codes EXCEPT
   (A) slaves could not own weapons.
   (B) slaves could not receive an education.
   (C) slaves could not testify against white people.
   (D) slaves could not be sold without their permission.

6. Free blacks in the American colonies tended to be black immigrants from the West Indies or
   (F) slaves who had earned their freedom.
   (G) runaway slaves.
   (H) slaves.
   (J) relatives of white people.

7. The machine that greatly increased the need for slaves was the
   (A) cotton gin.   (C) steam engine.
   (B) loom.   (D) water wheel.

8. Nat Turner, and the *Amistad*, are names associated with
   (F) plantations.   (H) colonial days.
   (G) slave revolts. (J) *Uncle Tom's Cabin*.

9. Fears by whites that a "race problem" would develop in the United States led to a project to transport volunteer free blacks to
   (A) England.   (C) South America.
   (B) Africa.   (D) Oregon.

10. Slavery became a national issue as
    (F) profits from cotton went up.
    (G) new states were admitted to the Union.
    (H) the railroad went West.
    (J) steel mills spread in the North.

11. To keep the balance of slave and free states, Missouri was admitted as a slave state, and Maine as a free state. This was known as
    (A) the Missouri Compromise.
    (B) the Articles of Confederation.
    (C) Lee's Measure.
    (D) the Freeport Doctrine.

12. The network of houses that hid slaves as they escaped North was known as
    (F) the sanctuary movement.
    (G) the underground railroad.
    (H) the abolition trail.
    (J) the drinking gourd.

13. Supporters of slavery won a major victory in the Supreme Court decision known as ____, which said that slaves were property.
    (A) *Brown vs. the Board of Topeka*
    (B) *Madison vs. Marbury*
    (C) the Dred Scott case
    (D) the Railroad Sleeping Car case

14. Abraham Lincoln's election to the presidency in 1860 infuriated Southerners because
    (F) he was from Illinois.
    (G) he was a third-party candidate and unknown.
    (H) he was an opponent of slavery.
    (J) he immediately declared war on the South.

> **STOP**

The Westward Movement

Directions: Match the date on the timeline with the correct event.

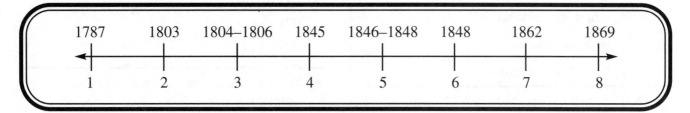

1787   1803   1804–1806   1845   1846–1848   1848   1862   1869

1   2   3   4   5   6   7   8

(A) The Northwest Ordinance provided government for the Northwest Territory.

(B) Lewis and Clark explored the northern part of the Louisiana Territory.

(C) War with Mexico resulted in the acquisition of California and the Southwest.

(D) The Homestead Act promised free land to settlers in the West.

(F) The nation's first transcontinental rail system was completed.

(G) The United States annexed Texas.

(H) The discovery of gold in California inspired the gold rush.

(J) The Louisiana Purchase opened a vast area beyond the Mississippi River to American settlers.

Directions: Match the column on the left with the column on the right.

9. Daniel Boone

10. the Old Northwest

11. Ordinance of 1785

12. Tecumseh

13. steamboats and railroads

14. the Adams-Onis Treaty

15. Louisiana Purchase

16. Jim Bridger, Kit Carson, Thomas Fitzpatrick, and Jedediah Smith

(A) encouraged the settlement of the Old Northwest

(B) territory divided into townships of 6 miles (9.7 kilometers) square (These townships were further divided into 36 sections, each 1 mile/1.6 kilometers square.)

(C) extends the United States territory from the Mississippi to the Rockies

(D) led a group of woodsmen from Tennessee through the Cumberland Gap into Kentucky

(F) worked to build an alliance of Indians to stop the invasion of white settlers

(G) "Mountain Men" who explored the Far West

(H) extended from the Ohio River north to the Great Lakes and from Pennsylvania west to the Mississippi River

(J) opened up Florida, and southern Mississippi and Alabama for settlement

➤ **STOP** ◄

Fine Arts: Music, Dance, and Theater

1. Which is not a category of musical instruments?

   (A) stringed instruments

   (B) guitar instruments

   (C) wind instruments

   (D) percussion instruments

2. Music is sound arranged into pleasing or interesting

   (F) pages.

   (G) CDs.

   (H) songs.

   (J) patterns.

3. _____ combines singing and orchestra music with drama.

   (A) Ballet

   (B) Concert

   (C) Choir

   (D) Opera

4. The music of people in Europe and the Americas is known as _____ music.

   (F) Eastern

   (G) Western

   (H) Southern

   (J) Northern

5. Which is NOT a form of classical music?

   (A) symphonies

   (B) operas

   (C) ballets

   (D) jazz

6. Where might you hear music?

   (F) sports events

   (G) parades

   (H) graduations

   (J) all of these

7. A musical sound is called a

   (A) song.

   (B) string.

   (C) tone.

   (D) chime.

8. What produces musical sounds in the human voice?

   (F) the mouth

   (G) the throat

   (H) the tongue

   (J) the vocal chords

9. One way a musician changes the pitch on a stringed instrument is to

   (A) pull the bow harder across the strings.

   (B) tighten the strings.

   (C) press down with his chin.

   (D) pluck the strings with his fingers.

10. Which stringed instrument does NOT belong?

    (F) violin   (H) harp

    (G) cello   (J) viola

11. Which are two types of woodwind instruments?

    (A) oboes and flutes

    (B) trumpets and trombones

    (C) strings and clarinets

    (D) brass and flutes

12. Which are reed instruments?

    (F) trombones and trumpets

    (G) flutes and piccolos

    (H) tubas and French horns

    (J) clarinets and saxophones

GO →

13. Dancing is an act of moving the body in _____, usually in time to _____.
    (A) beat/drums
    (B) rhythm/music
    (C) sound/clapping
    (D) tempo/orchestration

14. Dancing is both a(n) _____ and a form of recreation.
    (F) business   (H) art
    (G) play   (J) theater

15. Dance may tell a _____, set a mood, or express an emotion.
    (A) poem   (C) ballet
    (B) play   (D) story

16. Dancing is also a way to enjoy the company of friends. On the American frontier, _____ dancing was a chance for people to get together.
    (F) ballet   (H) square
    (G) jazz   (J) modern

17. For many people dancing is a form of
    (A) self-expression. (C) self-worship.
    (B) self-denial.   (D) self-employment.

18. There are two major kinds of dancing: theatrical and social. Which is NOT a kind of theatrical dancing?
    (F) tap dancing   (H) modern dance
    (G) ballet   (J) slam

19. Which is NOT one of the purposes of a curtain in theater?
    (A) to conceal or reveal the stage
    (B) to permit changes in scenery
    (C) to mark changes in place or time
    (D) to keep the theater warm

20. Which would NOT be found behind the scenes in a theater?
    (F) rehearsal and dressing rooms
    (G) lighting and sound booths
    (H) ticket box office
    (J) storage space for costumes, scenery, properties, and lighting instruments

21. Which is NOT part of the director's job?
    (A) working with technicians, and designers of scenery, lighting, and costumes
    (B) running concessions
    (C) casting the performers
    (D) supervising rehearsals

22. Which of the following is NOT a technical job in theater?
    (F) lighting
    (G) sound
    (H) cleaning
    (J) makeup

23. The person playing the part is the same as the character in the play.
    (A) True   (B) False

24. Scenery in a play includes the floor of the stage and the stage curtain.
    (A) True   (B) False

25. A flat is a rectangular wooden frame over which canvas is stretched, so the canvas can be painted.
    (A) True   (B) False

26. A scene in a script is the painted background.
    (A) True   (B) False

➤ **STOP** ◄

Directions: Choose the correct word for each blank.

Search Engines

A search engine on the _____ will search the general Web database for keywords
1

supplied by the _____. Some of the most popular search engines are Alta Vista
2

(http://www.altavista.com); Hotbot (http://www.hotbot.com); Lycos Power Search

(http://lycospro.lycos.com); Excite (http://www.excite.com); Yahoo! (http://www.yahoo.com);

and Infoseek (http://infoseek.go.com).

Meta-search engines search several _____ at once. In a meta-search engine, you
3

submit _____ in its search box, and it transmits your search simultaneously to most of the
4

popular search engines and their databases of Web _____. Within a few seconds, you get
5

back a compilation of results containing matching _____ from all of the search engines
6

queried. This can save you a lot of time and provide an overview of the kinds of _____
7

"out there" matching any term, phrase-in-quotes, or set of terms and phrases.

---

1. (A) keyboard   (B) machine   (C) Internet   (D) program

---

2. (F) computer   (G) user   (H) dictionary   (J) drive

---

3. (A) computers   (B) places   (C) databases   (D) schools

---

4. (F) keywords   (G) ideas   (H) numbers   (J) passwords

---

5. (A) drives   (B) pages   (C) screens   (D) words

---

6. (F) words   (G) ideas   (H) sites   (J) computers

---

7. (A) schools   (B) documents   (C) people   (D) librarians

GO →

Tips on Using Search Engines

- Avoid using single keywords. The keyword "health" for example will bring up documents on medicine, psychiatry, alternative medicine, mental health, and lifestyle.

- Use more advanced techniques such as enclosing phrases in _____—"health careers outlook"—and submitting phrases that employ _____ logic: healthANDcareersBUT NOTmedicine.

8

9

- Be careful about following "cool" _____ to other sites. Often these are advertisements and have little relation to what you're researching.

10

- Meta-search engines do not eliminate the need to learn how to search skillfully at least a few general Web searching _____ such as AltaVista, Infoseek, Excite, and Hotbot. Even _____ engines can overlook valuable sites.

11

12

8. (F) periods   (G) parentheses   (H) quotes   (J) brackets

9. (A) perfect   (B) strange   (C) math   (D) Boolean

10. (F) ways   (G) links   (H) jumps   (J) dudes

11. (A) databases   (B) keys   (C) tools   (D) computers

12. (F) meta-search   (G) car   (H) software   (J) American

GO →

Computers and Technology: Vocabulary *(cont.)*

Directions: Match the term on the left with the definition on the right.

13. Back/Forward

14. Boolean logic

15. Bookmark

16. Browsers

17. Domain

18. Download

19. Find

20. Frames

(A) way to store in your computer sites you wish to return to

(B) returns you to the document previously viewed; goes to the next document

(C) common ones are .edu (education), .gov (government agency), .net (network related), .com (commercial), .org (non-profit and research organizations)

(D) searches for word(s) keyed in document in screen only

(F) save to diskette

(G) way to combine terms using "AND," "OR," "AND NOT" and sometimes "NEAR"

(H) divides the screen into segments, each with a scroll bar as if it were as "window" within the window

(J) software programs that enable you to view WWW documents

---

21. Internet

22. Host

23. Link

24. Keyword

25. Meta-search engine

26. Modem

27. Storage devices

28. Mouse

(A) the vast collection of inter-connected networks

(B) search engines that automatically submit your keyword search to several other search tools and retrieve results from all their databases

(C) If you click on it, you automatically go to another site.

(D) hard disks, floppy disks, special compact discs called CD-ROMs, and tapes

(F) computer that provides Web documents to clients or users.

(G) an electronic device that allows computers to communicate over telephone lines

(H) a word searched for in a search command

(J) a palm-sized device that the computer operator moves about on a flat surface

Student Answer Sheets

Language Arts: Writing
Competencies
Pages: 25–26

Test

1. Ⓐ Ⓑ Ⓒ Ⓓ
2. Ⓕ Ⓖ Ⓗ Ⓙ
3. Ⓐ Ⓑ Ⓒ Ⓓ
4. Ⓕ Ⓖ Ⓗ Ⓙ
5. Ⓐ Ⓑ Ⓒ Ⓓ
6. Ⓕ Ⓖ Ⓗ Ⓙ
7. Ⓐ Ⓑ Ⓒ Ⓓ
8. Ⓕ Ⓖ Ⓗ Ⓙ
9. Ⓐ Ⓑ Ⓒ Ⓓ
10. Ⓕ Ⓖ Ⓗ Ⓙ
11. Ⓐ Ⓑ Ⓒ Ⓓ
12. Ⓕ Ⓖ Ⓗ Ⓙ
13. Ⓐ Ⓑ Ⓒ Ⓓ
14. Ⓕ Ⓖ Ⓗ Ⓙ
15. Ⓐ Ⓑ Ⓒ Ⓓ
16. Ⓕ Ⓖ Ⓗ Ⓙ
17. Ⓐ Ⓑ Ⓒ Ⓓ
18. Ⓕ Ⓖ Ⓗ Ⓙ
19. Ⓐ Ⓑ Ⓒ Ⓓ
20. Ⓕ Ⓖ Ⓗ Ⓙ

Language Arts: Reading
Competencies
Pages: 21–24

Test

1. Ⓐ Ⓑ Ⓒ Ⓓ
2. Ⓕ Ⓖ Ⓗ Ⓙ
3. Ⓐ Ⓑ Ⓒ Ⓓ
4. Ⓕ Ⓖ Ⓗ Ⓙ
5. Ⓐ Ⓑ Ⓒ Ⓓ
6. Ⓕ Ⓖ Ⓗ Ⓙ
7. Ⓐ Ⓑ Ⓒ Ⓓ
8. Ⓕ Ⓖ Ⓗ Ⓙ
9. Ⓐ Ⓑ Ⓒ Ⓓ
10. Ⓕ Ⓖ Ⓗ Ⓙ
11. Ⓐ Ⓑ Ⓒ Ⓓ

Language Arts: Reading
Competencies
Pages: 19–20

Test

1. Ⓐ Ⓑ
2. Ⓐ Ⓑ
3. Ⓐ Ⓑ
4. Ⓐ Ⓑ
5. Ⓐ Ⓑ
6. Ⓐ Ⓑ
7. Ⓐ Ⓑ Ⓒ Ⓓ
8. Ⓕ Ⓖ Ⓗ Ⓙ
9. Ⓐ Ⓑ Ⓒ Ⓓ
10. Ⓕ Ⓖ Ⓗ Ⓙ
11. Ⓐ Ⓑ Ⓒ Ⓓ
12. Ⓕ Ⓖ Ⓗ Ⓙ

Language Arts: Reading
Competencies
Pages: 15–18

Test

1. Ⓐ Ⓑ Ⓒ Ⓓ
2. Ⓕ Ⓖ Ⓗ Ⓙ
3. Ⓐ Ⓑ Ⓒ Ⓓ
4. Ⓕ Ⓖ Ⓗ Ⓙ
5. Ⓐ Ⓑ Ⓒ Ⓓ
6. Ⓕ Ⓖ Ⓗ Ⓙ
7. Ⓐ Ⓑ Ⓒ Ⓓ
8. Ⓕ Ⓖ Ⓗ Ⓙ

Student Answer Sheets (cont.)

Language Arts: Writing Competencies
Pages: 27–29

Sample Ⓐ Ⓑ Ⓒ Ⓓ

Test

1. Ⓐ Ⓑ Ⓒ Ⓓ
2. Ⓕ Ⓖ Ⓗ Ⓙ
3. Ⓐ Ⓑ Ⓒ Ⓓ
4. Ⓕ Ⓖ Ⓗ Ⓙ
5. Ⓐ Ⓑ Ⓒ Ⓓ
6. Ⓕ Ⓖ Ⓗ Ⓙ
7. Ⓐ Ⓑ Ⓒ Ⓓ
8. Ⓕ Ⓖ Ⓗ Ⓙ
9. Ⓐ Ⓑ Ⓒ Ⓓ
10. Ⓕ Ⓖ Ⓗ Ⓙ
11. Ⓐ Ⓑ Ⓒ Ⓓ
12. Ⓕ Ⓖ Ⓗ Ⓙ
13. Ⓐ Ⓑ Ⓒ Ⓓ
14. Ⓕ Ⓖ Ⓗ Ⓙ
15. Ⓐ Ⓑ Ⓒ Ⓓ
16. Ⓕ Ⓖ Ⓗ Ⓙ
17. Ⓐ Ⓑ Ⓒ Ⓓ
18. Ⓕ Ⓖ Ⓗ Ⓙ
19. Ⓐ Ⓑ Ⓒ Ⓓ
20. Ⓕ Ⓖ Ⓗ Ⓙ
21. Ⓐ Ⓑ Ⓒ Ⓓ

Language Arts: Writing Competencies
Pages: 30–31

Sample Ⓐ Ⓑ Ⓒ

Test

1. Ⓐ Ⓑ Ⓒ
2. Ⓕ Ⓖ Ⓗ
3. Ⓐ Ⓑ Ⓒ
4. Ⓕ Ⓖ Ⓗ
5. Ⓐ Ⓑ Ⓒ
6. Ⓕ Ⓖ Ⓗ
7. Ⓐ Ⓑ Ⓒ
8. Ⓕ Ⓖ Ⓗ
9. Ⓐ Ⓑ Ⓒ
10. Ⓕ Ⓖ Ⓗ
11. Ⓐ Ⓑ Ⓒ
12. Ⓕ Ⓖ Ⓗ
13. Ⓐ Ⓑ Ⓒ
14. Ⓕ Ⓖ Ⓗ

Language Arts: Writing Competencies
Pages: 32–33

Test

Student Answer Sheets *(cont.)*

Mathematics: Rational and Real Numbers
Page: 36

Test

#				
1.	Ⓐ	Ⓑ	Ⓒ	Ⓓ
2.	Ⓕ	Ⓖ	Ⓗ	Ⓙ
3.	Ⓐ	Ⓑ	Ⓒ	Ⓓ
4.	Ⓕ	Ⓖ	Ⓗ	Ⓙ
5.	Ⓐ	Ⓑ	Ⓒ	Ⓓ
6.	Ⓕ	Ⓖ	Ⓗ	Ⓙ
7.	Ⓐ	Ⓑ	Ⓒ	Ⓓ
8.	Ⓕ	Ⓖ	Ⓗ	Ⓙ
9.	Ⓐ	Ⓑ	Ⓒ	Ⓓ
10.	Ⓕ	Ⓖ	Ⓗ	Ⓙ
11.	Ⓐ	Ⓑ	Ⓗ	Ⓓ
12.	Ⓕ	Ⓖ	Ⓒ	Ⓓ
13.	Ⓐ	Ⓑ	Ⓒ	Ⓓ
14.	Ⓕ	Ⓖ	Ⓗ	Ⓙ

Mathematics: Rational and Real Numbers
Page: 37

Test

#				
1.	Ⓐ	Ⓑ	Ⓒ	Ⓓ
2.	Ⓕ	Ⓖ	Ⓗ	Ⓙ
3.	Ⓐ	Ⓑ	Ⓒ	Ⓓ
4.	Ⓕ	Ⓖ	Ⓗ	Ⓙ
5.	Ⓐ	Ⓑ	Ⓒ	Ⓓ
6.	Ⓕ	Ⓖ	Ⓗ	Ⓙ
7.	Ⓐ	Ⓑ	Ⓒ	Ⓓ
8.	Ⓕ	Ⓖ	Ⓗ	Ⓙ
9.	Ⓐ	Ⓑ	Ⓒ	Ⓓ
10.	Ⓕ	Ⓖ	Ⓗ	Ⓙ
11.	Ⓐ	Ⓑ	Ⓒ	Ⓓ
12.	Ⓕ	Ⓖ	Ⓗ	Ⓙ

Mathematics: Rational and Real Numbers
Page: 38

Test

#				
1.	Ⓐ	Ⓑ	Ⓒ	Ⓓ
2.	Ⓕ	Ⓖ	Ⓗ	Ⓙ
3.	Ⓐ	Ⓑ	Ⓒ	Ⓓ
4.	Ⓕ	Ⓖ	Ⓗ	Ⓙ
5.	Ⓐ	Ⓑ	Ⓒ	Ⓓ
6.	Ⓕ	Ⓖ	Ⓗ	Ⓙ
7.	Ⓐ	Ⓑ	Ⓒ	Ⓓ
8.	Ⓕ	Ⓖ	Ⓗ	Ⓙ
9.	Ⓐ	Ⓑ	Ⓒ	Ⓓ
10.	Ⓕ	Ⓖ	Ⓗ	Ⓙ
11.	Ⓐ	Ⓑ	Ⓒ	Ⓓ
12.	Ⓕ	Ⓖ	Ⓒ	Ⓓ
13.	Ⓐ	Ⓑ	Ⓒ	Ⓓ
14.	Ⓕ	Ⓖ	Ⓗ	Ⓙ

Mathematics: Geometry
Page: 39

Test

#				
1.	Ⓐ	Ⓑ	Ⓒ	Ⓓ
2.	Ⓐ	Ⓑ	Ⓒ	Ⓓ
3.	Ⓐ	Ⓑ	Ⓒ	Ⓓ
4.	Ⓕ	Ⓖ	Ⓗ	Ⓙ
5.	Ⓕ	Ⓖ	Ⓗ	Ⓙ
6.	Ⓕ	Ⓖ	Ⓗ	Ⓙ
7.	Ⓕ	Ⓖ	Ⓗ	Ⓙ
8.	Ⓐ	Ⓑ	Ⓒ	Ⓓ
9.	Ⓕ	Ⓖ	Ⓗ	Ⓙ
10.	Ⓐ	Ⓑ	Ⓒ	Ⓓ
11.	Ⓕ	Ⓖ	Ⓗ	Ⓙ
12.	Ⓐ	Ⓑ	Ⓒ	Ⓓ

Mathematics: Pre-Algebra
Page: 40

Test

1. A B C D
2. F G H J
3. A B C D
4. F G H J
5. A B C D
6. F G H J
7. A B C D
8. F G H J
9. A B C D
10. F G H J
11. A B C D
12. F G H J

Mathematics: Measurement
Page: 41

Test

1. A B C D
2. F G H J
3. A B C D
4. F G H J
5. A B C D
6. F G H J

Mathematics: Statistics and
Probability
Page: 42

Test

1. A B C D
2. F G H J
3. A B C D
4. F G H J
5. A B C D
6. F G H J
7. A B C D
8. F G H J

Mathematics: Statistics and
Probability
Page: 43

Test

1. A B C D
2. F G H J
3. A B C D
4. F G H J
5. A B C D
6. F G H J
7. A B C D
8. F G H J
9. A B C D
10. F G H J
11. A B C D
12. F G H J

Science: Geology
Page: 51

Test

	A/F	B/G	C/H	D/J
1.	A	B	C	D
2.	A	B	C	D
3.	A	B	C	D
4.	F	G	H	J
5.	F	G	H	J
6.	F	G	H	J
7.	A	B	C	D
8.	A	B	C	D
9.	A	B	C	D
10.	F	G	H	J
11.	F	G	H	J
12.	F	G	H	J
13.	A	B	C	D
14.	A	B	C	D
15.	A	B	C	D

Science: Atmospheric Studies
Pages: 48–50

Test

	A/F	B/G	C/H	D/J
1.	A	B	C	D
2.	F	G	H	J
3.	A	B	C	D
4.	F	G	H	J
5.	A	B	C	D
6.	F	G	H	J
7.	A	B	C	D
8.	F	G	H	J
9.	A	B	C	D
10.	F	G	H	J
11.	A	B	C	D
12.	F	G	H	J
13.	A	B	C	D
14.	F	G	H	J
15.	A	B	C	D
16.	F	G	H	J
17.	A	B	C	D
18.	F	G	H	J
19.	A	B		D
20.	A	B		
21.	A	B		

	A	B
22.	A	B
23.	A	B
24.	A	B
25.	A	B
26.	A	B
27.	A	B
28.	A	B

Science: General Science
Pages: 46–47

Sample

A B C D

Test

	A/F	B/G	C/H	D/J
1.	A	B	C	D
2.	F	G	H	J
3.	A	B	C	D
4.	F	G	H	J
5.	A	B	C	D
6.	F	G	H	J
7.	A	B	C	D
8.	F	G	H	J
9.	A	B	C	D
10.	F	G	H	J
11.	A	B	C	D
12.	F	G	H	J
13.	A	B	C	D
14.	F	G	H	J
15.	A	B	C	D
16.	F	G	H	J
17.	A	B	C	D
18.	F	G	H	J
19.	A	B	C	D
20.	F	G	H	J

Student Answer Sheets (cont.)

Social Studies: World History
Page: 60

Test

#				
1.	A	B	C	D
2.	F	G	H	J
3.	A	B	C	D
4.	F	G	H	J
5.	A	B	C	D
6.	F	G	H	J
7.	A	B	C	D
8.	F	G	H	J
9.	A	B	C	D
10.	F	G	H	J
11.	A	B	C	D
12.	F	G	H	J

Science: Reading
Pages: 56–57

Test

#				
1.	A	B	C	D
2.	A	B	H	J
3.	A	B	C	D
4.	F	G	H	J
5.	A	B	C	D
6.	F	G	H	J
7.	A	B	C	D

Science: Properties of Matter
Pages: 54–55

Test

#				
1.	A	B	C	D
2.	F	G	H	J
3.	A	B	C	D
4.	F	G	H	J
5.	A	B	C	D
6.	F	G	H	J
7.	A	B	C	D
8.	F	G	H	J
9.	A	B	C	D
10.	F	G	H	J
11.	A	B	C	
12.	A	B	C	
13.	A	B	C	
14.	A	B	C	
15.	A	B	C	
16.	A	B	C	
17.	A	B	C	
18.	A	B	C	
19.	A	B		
20.	A	B		
21.	A	B		
22.	A	B		

Science: Biology and Cells
Pages: 52–53

Test

#				
1.	A	B	C	D
2.	F	G	H	J
3.	A	B	C	D
4.	A	B	C	
5.	A	B	C	
6.	F	G	H	J
7.	A	B	C	D
8.	A	B		
9.	A	B		
10.	A	B		
11.	A	B		
12.	A	B		
13.	A	B		
14.	A	B		
15.	A	B		
16.	A	B		
17.	A	B		
18.	A	B		

Social Studies: World History
Page: 61

Test

#				
1.	Ⓐ	Ⓑ	Ⓒ	Ⓓ
2.	Ⓕ	Ⓖ	Ⓗ	Ⓙ
3.	Ⓐ	Ⓑ	Ⓒ	Ⓓ
4.	Ⓕ	Ⓖ	Ⓗ	Ⓙ
5.	Ⓐ	Ⓑ	Ⓒ	Ⓓ
6.	Ⓕ	Ⓖ	Ⓗ	Ⓙ
7.	Ⓐ	Ⓑ	Ⓒ	Ⓓ
8.	Ⓕ	Ⓖ	Ⓗ	Ⓙ
9.	Ⓐ	Ⓑ	Ⓒ	Ⓓ
10.	Ⓕ	Ⓖ	Ⓗ	Ⓙ
11.	Ⓐ	Ⓑ	Ⓒ	Ⓓ
12.	Ⓕ	Ⓖ	Ⓗ	Ⓙ
13.	Ⓐ	Ⓑ	Ⓒ	Ⓓ
14.	Ⓕ	Ⓖ	Ⓗ	Ⓙ
15.	Ⓐ	Ⓑ	Ⓒ	Ⓓ
16.	Ⓕ	Ⓖ	Ⓗ	Ⓙ
17.	Ⓐ	Ⓑ	Ⓒ	Ⓓ
18.	Ⓕ	Ⓖ	Ⓗ	Ⓙ
19.	Ⓐ	Ⓑ	Ⓒ	Ⓓ
20.	Ⓕ	Ⓖ	Ⓗ	Ⓙ
21.	Ⓐ	Ⓑ	Ⓒ	Ⓓ
22.	Ⓕ	Ⓖ	Ⓗ	Ⓙ
23.	Ⓐ	Ⓑ	Ⓒ	Ⓓ
24.	Ⓕ	Ⓖ	Ⓗ	Ⓙ
25.	Ⓐ	Ⓑ	Ⓒ	Ⓓ
26.	Ⓕ	Ⓖ	Ⓗ	Ⓙ
27.	Ⓐ	Ⓑ	Ⓒ	Ⓓ
28.	Ⓕ	Ⓖ	Ⓗ	Ⓙ
29.	Ⓐ	Ⓑ	Ⓒ	Ⓓ
30.	Ⓕ	Ⓖ	Ⓗ	Ⓙ
31.	Ⓐ	Ⓑ	Ⓒ	Ⓓ
32.	Ⓕ	Ⓖ	Ⓗ	Ⓙ

Social Studies: World History
Page: 62

Test

#				
1.	Ⓐ	Ⓑ	Ⓒ	Ⓓ
2.	Ⓕ	Ⓖ	Ⓗ	Ⓙ
3.	Ⓐ	Ⓑ	Ⓒ	Ⓓ
4.	Ⓕ	Ⓖ	Ⓗ	Ⓙ
5.	Ⓐ	Ⓑ	Ⓒ	Ⓓ
6.	Ⓕ	Ⓖ	Ⓗ	Ⓙ
7.	Ⓐ	Ⓑ	Ⓒ	Ⓓ
8.	Ⓕ	Ⓖ	Ⓗ	Ⓙ
9.	Ⓐ	Ⓑ	Ⓒ	Ⓓ
10.	Ⓕ	Ⓖ	Ⓗ	Ⓙ
11.	Ⓐ	Ⓑ	Ⓒ	Ⓓ
12.	Ⓕ	Ⓖ	Ⓗ	Ⓙ
13.	Ⓐ	Ⓑ	Ⓒ	Ⓓ
14.	Ⓕ	Ⓖ	Ⓗ	Ⓙ
15.	Ⓐ	Ⓑ	Ⓒ	Ⓓ
16.	Ⓕ	Ⓖ	Ⓗ	Ⓙ
17.	Ⓐ	Ⓑ	Ⓒ	Ⓓ
18.	Ⓕ	Ⓖ	Ⓗ	Ⓙ
19.	Ⓐ	Ⓑ	Ⓒ	Ⓓ
20.	Ⓕ	Ⓖ	Ⓗ	Ⓙ
21.	Ⓐ	Ⓑ	Ⓒ	Ⓓ
22.	Ⓕ	Ⓖ	Ⓗ	Ⓙ
23.	Ⓐ	Ⓑ	Ⓒ	Ⓓ
24.	Ⓕ	Ⓖ	Ⓗ	Ⓙ
25.	Ⓐ	Ⓑ	Ⓒ	Ⓓ
26.	Ⓕ	Ⓖ	Ⓗ	Ⓙ
27.	Ⓐ	Ⓑ	Ⓒ	Ⓓ
28.	Ⓕ	Ⓖ	Ⓗ	Ⓙ
29.	Ⓐ	Ⓑ	Ⓒ	Ⓓ
30.	Ⓕ	Ⓖ	Ⓗ	Ⓙ
31.	Ⓐ	Ⓑ	Ⓒ	Ⓓ
32.	Ⓕ	Ⓖ	Ⓗ	Ⓙ

Student Answer Sheets (cont.)

Social Studies: United States History
Pages: 66–67

Test

1.	Ⓐ	Ⓑ	Ⓒ	Ⓓ
2.	Ⓕ	Ⓖ	Ⓗ	Ⓙ
3.	Ⓐ	Ⓑ	Ⓒ	Ⓓ
4.	Ⓕ	Ⓖ	Ⓗ	Ⓙ
5.	Ⓐ	Ⓑ	Ⓒ	Ⓓ
6.	Ⓕ	Ⓖ	Ⓗ	Ⓙ
7.	Ⓐ	Ⓑ	Ⓒ	Ⓓ
8.	Ⓕ	Ⓖ	Ⓗ	Ⓙ
9.	Ⓐ	Ⓑ	Ⓒ	Ⓓ
10.	Ⓕ	Ⓖ	Ⓗ	Ⓙ
11.	Ⓐ	Ⓑ	Ⓒ	Ⓓ
12.	Ⓕ	Ⓖ	Ⓗ	Ⓙ
13.	Ⓐ	Ⓑ	Ⓒ	Ⓓ
14.	Ⓕ	Ⓖ	Ⓗ	Ⓙ
15.	Ⓐ	Ⓑ	Ⓒ	Ⓓ

Social Studies: United States History
Page: 65

Test

1.	Ⓐ	Ⓑ		
2.	Ⓐ	Ⓑ		
3.	Ⓐ	Ⓑ		
4.	Ⓐ	Ⓑ		
5.	Ⓐ	Ⓑ		
6.	Ⓕ	Ⓖ	Ⓗ	Ⓙ
7.	Ⓐ	Ⓑ	Ⓒ	Ⓓ
8.	Ⓕ	Ⓖ	Ⓗ	Ⓙ
9.	Ⓐ	Ⓑ	Ⓒ	Ⓓ
10.	Ⓕ	Ⓖ	Ⓗ	Ⓙ
11.	Ⓐ	Ⓑ	Ⓒ	Ⓓ
12.	Ⓕ	Ⓖ	Ⓗ	Ⓙ
13.	Ⓐ	Ⓑ	Ⓒ	Ⓓ
14.	Ⓕ	Ⓖ	Ⓗ	Ⓙ

Social Studies: World Geography
Pages: 63–64

Test

1.	Ⓐ	Ⓑ	Ⓒ	Ⓓ
2.	Ⓕ	Ⓖ	Ⓗ	Ⓙ
3.	Ⓐ	Ⓑ	Ⓒ	Ⓓ
4.	Ⓕ	Ⓖ	Ⓗ	Ⓙ
5.	Ⓐ	Ⓑ	Ⓒ	Ⓓ
6.	Ⓕ	Ⓖ	Ⓗ	Ⓙ
7.	Ⓐ	Ⓑ	Ⓒ	Ⓓ
8.	Ⓕ	Ⓖ	Ⓗ	Ⓙ
9.	Ⓐ	Ⓑ	Ⓒ	Ⓓ
10.	Ⓕ	Ⓖ	Ⓗ	Ⓙ
11.	Ⓐ	Ⓑ	Ⓒ	Ⓓ
12.	Ⓕ	Ⓖ	Ⓗ	Ⓙ
13.	Ⓐ	Ⓑ	Ⓒ	Ⓓ
14.	Ⓕ	Ⓖ	Ⓗ	Ⓙ
15.	Ⓐ	Ⓑ	Ⓒ	Ⓓ
16.	Ⓕ	Ⓖ	Ⓗ	Ⓙ
17.	Ⓐ	Ⓑ	Ⓒ	Ⓓ
18.	Ⓕ	Ⓖ	Ⓗ	Ⓙ
19.	Ⓐ	Ⓑ	Ⓒ	Ⓓ
20.	Ⓕ	Ⓖ	Ⓗ	Ⓙ
21.	Ⓐ	Ⓑ	Ⓒ	Ⓓ
22.	Ⓕ	Ⓖ	Ⓗ	Ⓙ
23.	Ⓐ	Ⓑ	Ⓒ	Ⓓ
24.	Ⓕ	Ⓖ	Ⓗ	Ⓙ
25.	Ⓐ	Ⓑ	Ⓒ	Ⓓ
26.	Ⓕ	Ⓖ	Ⓗ	Ⓙ

Social Studies: United States History
Page: 71

Test

1. Ⓐ Ⓑ Ⓒ Ⓓ
2. Ⓕ Ⓖ Ⓗ Ⓙ
3. Ⓐ Ⓑ Ⓒ Ⓓ
4. Ⓕ Ⓖ Ⓗ Ⓙ
5. Ⓐ Ⓑ Ⓒ Ⓓ
6. Ⓕ Ⓖ Ⓗ Ⓙ
7. Ⓐ Ⓑ Ⓒ Ⓓ
8. Ⓕ Ⓖ Ⓗ Ⓙ
9. Ⓐ Ⓑ Ⓒ Ⓓ
10. Ⓕ Ⓖ Ⓗ Ⓙ
11. Ⓐ Ⓑ Ⓒ Ⓓ
12. Ⓕ Ⓖ Ⓗ Ⓙ
13. Ⓐ Ⓑ Ⓒ Ⓓ
14. Ⓕ Ⓖ Ⓗ Ⓙ
15. Ⓐ Ⓑ Ⓒ Ⓓ
16. Ⓕ Ⓖ Ⓗ Ⓙ

Social Studies: United States History
Page: 70

Test

1. Ⓐ Ⓑ Ⓒ Ⓓ
2. Ⓕ Ⓖ Ⓗ Ⓙ
3. Ⓐ Ⓑ Ⓒ Ⓓ
4. Ⓕ Ⓖ Ⓗ Ⓙ
5. Ⓐ Ⓑ Ⓒ Ⓓ
6. Ⓕ Ⓖ Ⓗ Ⓙ
7. Ⓐ Ⓑ Ⓒ Ⓓ
8. Ⓕ Ⓖ Ⓗ Ⓙ
9. Ⓐ Ⓑ Ⓒ Ⓓ
10. Ⓕ Ⓖ Ⓗ Ⓙ
11. Ⓐ Ⓑ Ⓒ Ⓓ
12. Ⓕ Ⓖ Ⓗ Ⓙ
13. Ⓐ Ⓑ Ⓒ Ⓓ
14. Ⓕ Ⓖ Ⓗ Ⓙ

Social Studies: United States History
Page: 69

Test

1. Ⓐ Ⓑ
2. Ⓐ Ⓑ
3. Ⓐ Ⓑ
4. Ⓐ Ⓑ
5. Ⓐ Ⓑ
6. Ⓐ Ⓑ
7. Ⓐ Ⓑ
8. Ⓐ Ⓑ
9. Ⓐ Ⓑ
10. Ⓐ Ⓑ
11. Ⓐ Ⓑ
12. Ⓐ Ⓑ

Social Studies: United States History
Page: 68

Test

1. Ⓐ Ⓑ Ⓒ Ⓓ
2. Ⓕ Ⓖ Ⓗ Ⓙ
3. Ⓐ Ⓑ Ⓒ Ⓓ
4. Ⓕ Ⓖ Ⓗ Ⓙ
5. Ⓐ Ⓑ Ⓒ Ⓓ
6. Ⓕ Ⓖ Ⓗ Ⓙ
7. Ⓐ Ⓑ Ⓒ Ⓓ
8. Ⓕ Ⓖ Ⓗ Ⓙ
9. Ⓐ Ⓑ Ⓒ Ⓓ
10. Ⓕ Ⓖ Ⓗ Ⓙ
11. Ⓐ Ⓑ Ⓒ Ⓓ
12. Ⓕ Ⓖ Ⓗ Ⓙ
13. Ⓐ Ⓑ Ⓒ Ⓓ
14. Ⓕ Ⓖ Ⓗ Ⓙ
15. Ⓐ Ⓑ Ⓒ Ⓓ
16. Ⓕ Ⓖ Ⓗ Ⓙ

Fine Arts: Music, Dance, and Theater
Pages: 72–73

Test

1. Ⓐ Ⓑ Ⓒ Ⓓ
2. Ⓕ Ⓖ Ⓗ Ⓙ
3. Ⓐ Ⓑ Ⓒ Ⓓ
4. Ⓕ Ⓖ Ⓗ Ⓙ
5. Ⓐ Ⓑ Ⓒ Ⓓ
6. Ⓕ Ⓖ Ⓗ Ⓙ
7. Ⓐ Ⓑ Ⓒ Ⓓ
8. Ⓕ Ⓖ Ⓗ Ⓙ
9. Ⓐ Ⓑ Ⓒ Ⓓ
10. Ⓕ Ⓖ Ⓗ Ⓙ
11. Ⓐ Ⓑ Ⓒ Ⓓ
12. Ⓕ Ⓖ Ⓗ Ⓙ
13. Ⓐ Ⓑ Ⓒ Ⓓ
14. Ⓕ Ⓖ Ⓗ Ⓙ
15. Ⓐ Ⓑ Ⓒ Ⓓ
16. Ⓕ Ⓖ Ⓗ Ⓙ
17. Ⓐ Ⓑ Ⓒ Ⓓ
18. Ⓕ Ⓖ Ⓗ Ⓙ
19. Ⓐ Ⓑ Ⓒ Ⓓ
20. Ⓕ Ⓖ Ⓗ Ⓙ
21. Ⓐ Ⓑ Ⓒ Ⓓ
22. Ⓕ Ⓖ Ⓗ Ⓙ
23. Ⓐ Ⓑ Ⓒ Ⓓ
24. Ⓐ Ⓑ
25. Ⓐ Ⓑ
26. Ⓐ Ⓑ

Computers and Technology:
Vocabulary
Pages: 74–76

Test

1. Ⓐ Ⓑ Ⓒ Ⓓ
2. Ⓕ Ⓖ Ⓗ Ⓙ
3. Ⓐ Ⓑ Ⓒ Ⓓ
4. Ⓕ Ⓖ Ⓗ Ⓙ
5. Ⓐ Ⓑ Ⓒ Ⓓ
6. Ⓕ Ⓖ Ⓗ Ⓙ
7. Ⓐ Ⓑ Ⓒ Ⓓ
8. Ⓕ Ⓖ Ⓗ Ⓙ
9. Ⓐ Ⓑ Ⓒ Ⓓ
10. Ⓕ Ⓖ Ⓗ Ⓙ
11. Ⓐ Ⓑ Ⓒ Ⓓ
12. Ⓕ Ⓖ Ⓗ Ⓙ
13. Ⓐ Ⓑ Ⓒ Ⓓ
14. Ⓕ Ⓖ Ⓗ Ⓙ
15. Ⓐ Ⓑ Ⓒ Ⓓ
16. Ⓕ Ⓖ Ⓗ Ⓙ
17. Ⓐ Ⓑ Ⓒ Ⓓ
18. Ⓕ Ⓖ Ⓗ Ⓙ
19. Ⓐ Ⓑ Ⓒ Ⓓ
20. Ⓕ Ⓖ Ⓗ Ⓙ
21. Ⓐ Ⓑ Ⓒ Ⓓ
22. Ⓕ Ⓖ Ⓗ Ⓙ
23. Ⓐ Ⓑ Ⓒ Ⓓ
24. Ⓕ Ⓖ Ⓗ Ⓙ
25. Ⓐ Ⓑ Ⓒ Ⓓ
26. Ⓕ Ⓖ Ⓗ Ⓙ
27. Ⓐ Ⓑ Ⓒ Ⓓ
28. Ⓕ Ⓖ Ⓗ Ⓙ

Language Arts: Writing
Competencies
Pages: 25–26

Test

1.	B
2.	G
3.	C
4.	F
5.	B
6.	F
7.	F
8.	J
9.	F
10.	G
11.	B
12.	G
13.	B
14.	F
15.	J
16.	G
17.	F
18.	H
19.	C
20.	F

Language Arts: Reading
Competencies
Pages: 21–24

Test

1.	C
2.	H
3.	B
4.	H
5.	D
6.	G
7.	D
8.	J
9.	F
10.	F
11.	D

Language Arts: Reading
Competencies
Pages: 19–20

Test

1.	B
2.	B
3.	B
4.	A
5.	B
6.	B
7.	B
8.	H
9.	B
10.	G
11.	D
12.	H

Language Arts: Reading
Competencies
Pages: 15–18

Test

1.	B
2.	H
3.	D
4.	J
5.	B
6.	H
7.	A
8.	J

Language Arts: Writing Competencies
Pages: 27–29

Sample: Ⓐ Ⓑ **●** Ⓓ (C)

Test

#	A / F	B / G	C / H	D / J
1.	Ⓐ	**●**	Ⓒ	Ⓓ
2.	Ⓕ	Ⓖ	**●**	Ⓙ
3.	**●**	Ⓖ	Ⓒ	Ⓓ
4.	Ⓕ	Ⓖ	**●**	Ⓙ
5.	Ⓐ	Ⓑ	**●**	Ⓓ
6.	Ⓕ	Ⓖ	Ⓗ	**●**
7.	Ⓐ	**●**	Ⓒ	Ⓓ
8.	**●**	Ⓖ	Ⓗ	Ⓙ
9.	Ⓐ	**●**	Ⓒ	Ⓓ
10.	Ⓕ	**●**	Ⓗ	Ⓙ
11.	Ⓐ	Ⓑ	**●**	Ⓓ
12.	Ⓕ	**●**	Ⓗ	Ⓙ
13.	**●**	Ⓑ	Ⓒ	Ⓓ
14.	Ⓕ	Ⓖ	**●**	Ⓙ
15.	**●**	Ⓑ	Ⓒ	Ⓓ
16.	Ⓕ	Ⓖ	**●**	Ⓙ
17.	Ⓐ	Ⓑ	Ⓒ	**●**
18.	Ⓕ	**●**	Ⓗ	Ⓙ
19.	Ⓐ	Ⓑ	Ⓒ	**●**
20.	Ⓕ	Ⓖ	**●**	Ⓙ
21.	Ⓐ	**●**	Ⓒ	Ⓓ

Language Arts: Writing Competencies
Pages: 30–31

Sample: **●** Ⓑ Ⓒ (A)

Test

#	A / F	B / G	C / H
1.	Ⓐ	**●**	Ⓒ
2.	Ⓕ	**●**	Ⓗ
3.	**●**	Ⓑ	Ⓒ
4.	**●**	Ⓖ	Ⓗ
5.	**●**	Ⓑ	Ⓒ
6.	**●**	Ⓖ	Ⓗ
7.	**●**	Ⓑ	Ⓒ
8.	**●**	Ⓖ	Ⓗ
9.	Ⓐ	**●**	Ⓒ
10.	**●**	Ⓖ	Ⓗ
11.	Ⓐ	**●**	Ⓒ
12.	Ⓕ	**●**	Ⓗ
13.	**●**	Ⓑ	Ⓒ
14.	Ⓕ	**●**	Ⓗ

Language Arts: Writing Competencies
Pages: 32–33

Test

Answers will vary.

_____

_____

_____

_____

_____

_____

_____

_____

_____

_____

_____

_____

Answer Key (cont.)

Mathematics: Rational and Real Numbers
Page: 36

Test

1.	B
2.	F
3.	C
4.	J
5.	F
6.	G
7.	B
8.	H
9.	J
10.	G
11.	B
12.	G
13.	A
14.	H

Mathematics: Rational and Real Numbers
Page: 37

Test

1.	C
2.	H
3.	A
4.	J
5.	B
6.	G
7.	D
8.	H
9.	C
10.	G
11.	B
12.	J

Mathematics: Rational and Real Numbers
Page: 38

Test

1.	C
2.	F
3.	B
4.	F
5.	B
6.	G
7.	C
8.	F
9.	F
10.	G
11.	J
12.	J
13.	G
14.	H

Mathematics: Geometry
Page: 39

Test

1.	A
2.	G
3.	C
4.	H
5.	D
6.	F
7.	B
8.	J
9.	B
10.	J
11.	C
12.	F

Answer Key *(cont.)*

Mathematics: Pre-Algebra
Page: 40

Test
1. B
2. F
3. B
4. F
5. C
6. G
7. A
8. H
9. C
10. H
11. B
12. F

Mathematics: Measurement
Page: 41

Test
1. B
2. G
3. C
4. F
5. C
6. J

Mathematics: Statistics and Probability
Page: 42

Test
1. D
2. F
3. D
4. J
5. A
6. F
7. C
8. H

Mathematics: Statistics and Probability
Page: 43

Test
1. B
2. F
3. C
4. H
5. A
6. G
7. B
8. H
9. A
10. G
11. A
12. F

Science: Geology
Page: 51

Test

1. 2. 3. 4. 5. 6. 7. 8. 9. 10. 11. 12. 13. 14. 15.

Science: Atmospheric Studies
Pages: 48–50

Test

1. 2. 3. 4. 5. 6. 7. 8. 9. 10. 11. 12. 13. 14. 15. 16. 17. 18. 19. 20. 21.

22. 23. 24. 25. 26. 27. 28.

Science: General Science
Pages: 46–47

Sample

Test

1. 2. 3. 4. 5. 6. 7. 8. 9. 10. 11. 12. 13. 14. 15. 16. 17. 18. 19. 20.

Answer Key (cont.)

Social Studies: World History
Page: 60

Test

1. B
2. F
3. B
4. H
5. C
6. F
7. B
8. H
9. D
10. G
11. A
12. G

Science: Reading
Pages: 56–57

Test

1. A
2. G
3. C
4. F
5. B
6. H
7. B

Science: Properties of Matter
Pages: 54–55

Test

1. C
2. H
3. B
4. J
5. C
6. G
7. A
8. G
9. C
10. F
11. A
12. F
13. C
14. F
15. C
16. G
17. C
18. G
19. A
20. F
21. B
22. F

Science: Biology and Cells
Pages: 52–53

Test

1. D
2. G
3. A
4. G
5. C
6. H
7. C
8. G
9. A
10. G
11. A
12. G
13. A
14. F
15. B
16. G
17. A
18. F

Social Studies: World History
Page: 61

Test

1.   2.   3.   4.   5.   6.   7.   8.   9.   10.   11.   12.   13.   14.   15.   16.   17.   18.   19.   20.   21.   22.   23.

24.   25.   26.   27.   28.   29.   30.   31.   32.

Social Studies: World History
Page: 62

Test

1.   2.   3.   4.   5.   6.   7.   8.   9.   10.   11.   12.   13.   14.   15.   16.   17.   18.   19.   20.   21.   22.   23.

24.   25.   26.   27.   28.   29.   30.   31.   32.

Social Studies: World Geography
Pages: 63–64

Test

#	A/F	B/G	C/H	D/J
1.	A	●	C	D
2.	●	G	H	J
3.	A	B	C	●
4.	F	●	H	J
5.	A	B	●	D
6.	F	G	●	J
7.	A	B	C	●
8.	F	●	H	J
9.	●	B	C	J
10.	●	G	H	D
11.	A	B	●	J
12.	F	G	●	D
13.	A	B	●	J
14.	●	G	H	D
15.	●	B	C	●
16.	F	G	●	●
17.	A	●	H	●
18.	F	B	C	●
19.	A	G	H	●
20.	F	B	C	●
21.	A	G	●	D
22.	●	G	H	J
23.	●	B	C	D

Social Studies: United States History
Page: 65

Test

#	A/F	B/G	C/H	D/J
1.	●	B		
2.	●	B		
3.	A	●	H	D
4.	A	●	●	J
5.	A	B	C	D
6.	F	●	●	J
7.	A	●	H	D
8.	F	G	C	J
9.	A	B	●	D
10.	●	G	H	●
11.	●	B	C	●
12.	F	G	H	●
13.	A	●	C	J
14.	F	●	H	J

24. (F)
25. (A)
26. (F)

24. ● (H) (J)
25. ● (C) (D)
26. (G) ● (J)

Social Studies: United States History
Pages: 66–67

Test

#	A/F	B/G	C/H	D/J
1.	A	B	C	●
2.	F	●	H	J
3.	A	●	C	D
4.	F	G	H	●
5.	A	●	C	D
6.	F	●	●	J
7.	A	●	●	D
8.	F	●	H	J
9.	A	●	C	●
10.	F	B	H	J
11.	A	●	C	D
12.	F	●	●	J
13.	A	G	●	D
14.	F	B	H	●
15.	A	●	C	D

Answer Key *(cont.)*

Social Studies: United States History — Page 68

Test

1. B	2. J	3. D	4. F	5. C	6. G	7. A	8. H
9. A	10. G	11. D	12. H	13. C	14. F	15. B	16. J

Social Studies: United States History — Page 69

Test

1. A	2. B	3. B	4. A	5. A	6. B
7. A	8. B	9. A	10. B	11. B	12. A

Social Studies: United States History — Page 70

Test

1. B	2. H	3. D	4. F	5. D	6. F	7. A
8. G	9. B	10. G	11. A	12. G	13. H	14. H

Social Studies: United States History — Page 71

Test

1. A	2. J	3. B	4. G	5. C	6. H	7. D	8. F
9. D	10. H	11. B	12. F	13. A	14. J	15. C	16. G

Answer Key (cont.)

Fine Arts: Music, Dance, and Theater
Pages: 72–73

Test

1.	B
2.	J
3.	D
4.	G
5.	D
6.	J
7.	C
8.	J
9.	B
10.	H
11.	A
12.	J
13.	B
14.	H
15.	D
16.	H
17.	A
18.	J
19.	D
20.	H
21.	A
22.	H
23.	D
24.	(filled)
25.	A
26.	(filled)

Computers and Technology: Vocabulary
Pages: 74–76

Test

1.	C
2.	G
3.	C
4.	F
5.	B
6.	F
7.	B
8.	H
9.	D
10.	G
11.	C
12.	F
13.	B
14.	G
15.	A
16.	J
17.	C
18.	F
19.	D
20.	H
21.	A
22.	F
23.	C
24.	H
25.	B
26.	G
27.	D
28.	J